WITHDRAWN
UTSA LIBRARIES

CRISIS
INTERVENTION
AND HOW
IT WORKS

CRISIS INTERVENTION AND HOW IT WORKS

Romaine V. Edwards, M.S.W.

CHARLES C THOMAS • PUBLISHER
Springfield • Illinois • U.S.A.

Published and Distributed Throughout the World by
CHARLES C THOMAS ● PUBLISHER
Bannerstone House
301-327 East Lawrence Avenue, Springfield, Illinois, U.S.A.

© *1977, by* CHARLES C THOMAS ● PUBLISHER
ISBN 0-398-03580-6
Library of Congress Catalog Card Number: 76-16566

With THOMAS BOOKS *careful attention is given to all details of
manufacturing and design. It is the Publisher's desire to present books that are
satisfactory as to their physical qualities and artistic possibilities and
appropriate for their particular use.* THOMAS BOOKS *will be true to those
laws of quality that assure a good name and good will.*

Printed in the United States of America
R-11

Library of Congress Cataloging in Publication Data

Edwards, Romaine V
    Crisis intervention and how it works.

    Includes index.
    1. Crisis intervention (Psychiatry) I. Title.
[DNLM: 1. Crisis intervention. 2. Voluntary workers--
Education. 3. Psychiatric aides--Education. 4. Com-
munity mental health services. WM30 E265c]
RC480.6.E38   362.2'2   76-16566
ISBN 0-398-03580-6

to my husband, Jerry Edwards,
whose persistence and determination
made all of this possible

ACKNOWLEDGMENTS

ACKNOWLEDGMENTS for any book are difficult because so many people prove helpful in its writing. Acknowledgments for this book are especially difficult because this description of the A-B-C Method of helping fellow human beings in times of emotional crisis is the culmination of my life's work. All of my life on campuses, in social work, in institutions, and through countless community organizations has added to my understanding of human crisis and contributed to my insight about how others can be helped to cope with the very real traumas that camp uninvited in the center of their consciousness. There is scarcely a person I've known in my life who has not played a part in my understanding of what's real and what's meaningful in others. I could not possibly begin to list those who have played even a very direct role in the preparation of this book. But facing the fact that only a few can be mentioned, I would like to say thank you in a very special way to some very special people.

No other person was as important to this undertaking as my husband, Jerry. It is so literally true that without him, this book could never have been written. His constant encouragement and support kept my eye on the mark. The book would also not have been possible without my children John and Lea, who presented me with many crises in their growth and development, and understood as children that I needed time to develop the manuscript. Lea read the first three chapters at age 12 and gave a profound interpretation of the Method. And speaking of relatives, I would like to give special thanks to my parents, Eunice and William J. Moore, who guided me through life and gave me a philosophy that all things are possible if you believe in yourself, and to Shirley Burch, my niece, whose admiration and emulation I could not betray.

I needed a great deal of professional help from a variety of disciplines to verify countless small, but important, technical points. I have been gratified by the unselfish time and advise from a number of professionals who believe in paraprofessional counseling and who were not in any way threatened by helping lift the mystical curtain to what we know about crisis intervention.

I extend special thanks to Warren L. Jones, M.D., Psychiatrist, who introduced me to the Method and who was the foundation of experiential learning and theoretical teaching for me and my staff at the Pasadena Mental Health Center and the staff aides, who utilized the method constantly so that it became refined to what it is today. Other professionals include: Dr. Edwin Krauser, Psychologist; Dr. Paul Pretzel, Psychologist and Suicidologist; Dr. Margaret Bennett, Psychologist; Basil Clyman, M.D.; George Lundberg, M.D.; Jim Johnson, M.D.; Judith Krauser, M.S.W.; Attorney Charles Johnson of Pasadena; Bruce H. Woolley, Pharm.D.; Bruce Clayton and Alex Arrendondo of Phoenix, Arizona.

There are those who helped in other special ways. Patricia A. Tate and Laura Galaviz who typed the manuscript over and over are two such persons.

At a last acknowledgment I would like to say that I am indebted to Nat Read, a sensitive friend and talented writer, who hammered through every word and sentence with me, forming the transition from life's philosophy to printed word.

There are so many others who know how much they have meant to my professional life, who know that they are remembered and treasured, even though their names are not specifically mentioned here. To all the above, listed and unlisted, who helped me cope with the very real crisis of writing my first book, thank you.

CONTENTS

Page

Acknowledgments vii

Chapter

ONE. WHAT'S A PARAPROFESSIONAL LIKE YOU DOING IN A
WORLD LIKE THIS? 3

TWO. HOW DOES IT WORK? 8

THREE. THE ABC METHOD IS THE KEY 16

FOUR. A IS FOR ACQUIRING 22

FIVE. B IS FOR BOILING DOWN 28

SIX. C IS FOR COPING 34

SEVEN. IT ALL COMES TOGETHER HERE 39

EIGHT. SUICIDE AND HOMICIDE — THE ULTIMATE CRISES 42

NINE. SUBSTANCE ABUSE: ALCOHOL AND DRUGS
MEAN PROBLEMS.................................. 48

TEN. ETHICS AND LEGALITY 57

ELEVEN. THE BUILDING BLOCKS OF A COUNSELING SERVICE 64

Index 75

CRISIS
INTERVENTION
AND HOW
IT WORKS

CHAPTER ONE

WHAT'S A PARAPROFESSIONAL LIKE YOU DOING IN A WORLD LIKE THIS?

SIGMUND Freud was the granddaddy shrink of all time; when he fathered the new profession of psychiatry, he put an end to a beautiful thing: Ordinary people quit thinking they could help other ordinary people. Freud slipped into the world's awareness, and that Freudian slip divided the civilized world into two classes: There were those on the couch and those seated beside it. Those beside the couch had a college degree, topped by a medical license, topped by an internship and residency. Those on the couch had problems.

Fortunately, after a few generations of that sort of "shrinker vs. shrinkee" society, it suddenly dawned upon someone that maybe a dozen years of training were not needed to help some fellow humans with some of their human problems. Using the magical knowledge of Doctor Freud et al., ordinary folk could be trained to administer mental first aid in the same way that trained medics administer physical first aid.

The discovery that lay people could be trained to help other lay people with their problems meant a lot of exciting things. For one thing, not everybody who had lots of problems was someone who also had lots of money; so now a community could offer a free alternative to many people who had not any alternative before.

For another thing, the professional psychiatrist could now delegate some of his work. There did not need to be one professional for every problem. Thus an awful lot more people could be helped.

And now, people with medium-sized problems — problems not chronic enough for the psychiatrist's couch — had some place to go.

Twenty-four hour service could now be established in every decent-sized community. It turned out to be easier to sign up dedicated people for an all-night shift than the $50,000-a-year psychiatrist who had been counseling all day anyway. For years, people had been asked to schedule their personal crises between 9:00 and 5:00 on weekdays. At last, help was available at the time of the problem.

Another breakthrough for paraprofessional training was that peers could be taught to counsel peers. There no longer had to be educational gap or a cultural gap or an ethnic gap or a language gap between counseler and client. Student could counsel student, senior citizen could counsel senior citizen, inmate could counsel inmate and cop could counsel cop.

This breakthrough did not mean that the paraprofessional could now take the place of the professional. Not at all. The professional is needed more than ever now as a trainer of lay counselors and as a backup to treat the many, many cases who need the kind of help that only a trained, competent professional can give. Paraprofessional counseling is *not* a substitute for psychologists and psychiatrists. It is a supplement to professional help. Paraprofessional help extends the reach of professionals and at the same time frees the professional for the cases where he is needed most.

When a soldier falls on the battlefield, a medic or corpsman rushes to his aid. This paraprofessional sizes up the disabled man's condition. If an electrical charge has stopped his breathing, the medic can administer mouth-to-mouth resuscitation, restoring his breathing and thus overcoming the life-and-death crisis until the injured man can be brought to a physician's care behind the lines. Thus the paraprofessional saved the soldier's life and relayed him to the professional for further treatment and healing.

Or perhaps the fallen soldier's legs are broken and twisted. The medic can immobilize the fractures while the man is being rushed to a doctor's attention. Thus he has not cured the wounded man, but he has kept his wounds from getting worse until the soldier gets to the physician.

Or maybe the fallen soldier just fainted. In that case, the medic may administer first aid on the scene and return the man to duty without ever calling upon the professional skills of a doctor.

All of these medical situations have their counterparts in the psychological field. A paraprofessional is not a pro, but then again, every psychological splinter and bruise may not need a pro. The paraprofessional refers many problems to professional counselors and he refers many others to physicians. But surprisingly, or maybe not so surprisingly, the majority of the large and small problems that fellow human beings lay on the paraprofessional, he can handle all by himself, without ever involving the skills and time of a professional.

Very often, the problems brought to the paraprofessional are life-and-death problems, and the lay counselor's record in dealing with these extreme situations is proof of the paraprofessional theory. What more dramatic proof could one demand than the record of preserving life itself?

listener: Hello, San Gabriel Hotline.
caller: I'm holding a gun to my head and I'm going to kill myself.
listener: Please put the gun down. I'm only 16 and it frightens me.
caller: Gosh, I'm sorry. I didn't mean to scare you.

With this beginning, a high school volunteer in California broke the tension of a man threatening suicide, and before the call was over, the caller had decided to consult a psychiatrist when professional offices opened the next morning.

That call is not at all unusual. Hundreds of suicidal calls are handled every single night by hotline volunteers at telephone centers around the country. And hundreds of suicidal clients are counseled in face-to-face sessions at free clinics and paraprofessional counseling centers every day.

The suicidal and homicidal clients are the most dramatic and publicized calls on the skill of the non-degreed counselors. At the other end of the spectrum are the preteen callers with their first real love problems. And in between lie the thousands of big/little, tragic/comic problems that are pressing in enough on someone to convince them to call for help.

Paraprofessional counselors! All too many people doubt that it can happen. People are too conditioned to the hang-up that only a sheep skin and shingle can qualify mortal man or woman to help his fellow human being. Baloney! Think of all the scrapes and fevers we treat ourselves!

The plain truth is that paraprofessional counselors can help; they've been proving that by the thousands now for years, helping literally millions of people with problems that, though they seem large or small to us, were problem enough to someone else to warrant his seeking help.

When I consult with new organizations, I look around at a room full of sceptics. Written across every brow in the house is a not-too-well-concealed look of "I don't believe it can work!" Bear in mind that these are the very volunteers that signed up to help, and *they* don't think that they can really carry it off. Imagine what the others must think .... the ones who did not volunteer to be paraprofessional counselors!

The way I prove — and prove in a hurry — that the method actually works is to have them role-play, using a dummy telephone in a mock counseling room situation. I start the group out role-playing as soon as I've taught them enough of the ABC Method for them to put into use. One person acts as the counselor and another acts as a client with a problem, and away they go.

The sessions are beautiful. Every person in the room is out to prove that the Method will not work, that there is no help for personal problems this side of the $50-an-hour psychiatrist's couch. During all of their lives, they've been taught by society that only a professional can deal with the problems of his or her fellow human beings, and these volunteers are determined to prove that what they've been taught was right. They fight for the preservation of the fable by throwing into their role-playing the toughest problems they can conjure up. Their imaginations go wild with super-tough problems, and every role-playing pitch that they throw is a curve.

But what happens? The method wins hands down, and it wins every time. If it did not work, I wouldn't be writing this book. If it did not work, there wouldn't be the hundreds of telephone hotlines around the country, staffed by thousands of paraprofessionals, helping millions of callers. If it did not work, there wouldn't be the hundreds of walk-in, face-to-face counseling centers across the country, staffed again by competent paraprofessionals. While it is true that not all of the hotlines and counseling centers use the ABC Method, they use techniques of various names that are similar.

Paraprofessional counseling is here to stay. It is here because there is a crying need for people to help other people, and it is here because it works!

aide: What happened most recently that made you call us?

client: What happened? There are so many things that have happened in my life I don't know where to begin. But last night I got word that my Father has cancer, and my Mother would like to bring the family up here. I don't think I can take any more because I have enough of my own family.

aide: You mean responsibility for the people in your home?

client: I just couldn't take the pressure. I don't know whether that's responsibility. It's just the pressure would be too much.

aide: You said you were fearful last night your Father has cancer. Do you know for certain that your Father has cancer?

client: Yes, he has cancer. My Mother wants to bring him out here, but I just can't have him out here.

CHAPTER TWO

HOW DOES IT WORK?

HOW can a nonprofessional be trained to treat the mental health of his fellow man? How can life and death and mental adjustment be trusted to a housewife or student? With all of the brilliant psychiatrists and psychologists in this country, aren't our mental institutions still crammed to their limits? So, what presumptuous soul would pretend that amateurs are part of an answer that even the best professionals have not been able to reach?

I do.

Ordinary people are being trained to supplement the professional mental health care, and the record of these lay staff members over almost a decade of service proves the point. How is it possible?

It is possible because the paraprofessional knows his bounds. He knows his capabilities and makes the most of them, but he is equally aware of his limitations. It is possible because of the depth of compassion and understanding that most of us have but have never had a chance to channel and use systematically. And it is possible, because the paraprofessional is using a *professional counseling method*, developed by the best of professional psychiatrists, and backed up by professional resources.

Like his medical counterpart, the psychological paraprofessional knows what cases to refer to the professional and what to do until the professional arrives. But here is where the medical and psychological analogy ends: The medical paraprofessional administers the treatment himself while the psychological counselor helps the "patient" to administer self-treatment.

The variations of mental and psychological problems are infinitely more varied and complex than the range of physical ailments. But the solution for a caller's problems is going to have to come from the person who best knows those problems and their alternative solutions, and that is the client. So the paraprofessional does not have to learn a "pressure point" or "first aid technique" for every single psychological hang-up. Instead, we teach the paraprofessional a *method,* and he uses that method to work through each client's plea for help.

In years gone by there were other helping hands, other external resources to turn to. A person was part of a more tightly-knit family group then, and there were sympathetic relatives within a few miles. There were trusted friends, whose bonds had been welded by many years of close associations. And, of course, there was the family physician and the local clergyman.

Today's society has scattered the family to long distance outposts across the country. If we ourselves do not move from house to house and town to town, our neighbors do, so the net effect is the same: We just do not have time to build the bonds of friendship that our parents and grandparents did. Long gone is the family physician with his house calls and patient ear, and in many cases today's creature has no spiritual advisor in his life either.

Unable to lay himself open to a strange face and unable to "turn himself in" to a face-to-face counselor, he now has a logical and convenient starting point for external help. He can take his problems to his end of the phone, saving his ego and his anonymity, but still getting the steadying hand he needs. Later, when he comes to trust the paraprofessional system, he can come in for face-to-face counseling. How logical it is to use the familiar telephone to open communications with a source of help! No office hours. No appointment necessary.

Or maybe the problems were taken in person to a free clinic or other counseling service in the first place. The fact remains that today's troubled soul does not have the traditional sources of strength that were drawn upon by his parents and grandparents. Instead, he is taking his problems — by phone or in person — to strangers whom he thinks might be able to help him. And they are helping. They are viable alternatives to the clergy and relatives who helped yesteryear's afflicted and, in many cases, they are better. They are as much a part of today as the family pastor and kindly aunt were a part of yesterday. The competent training of today's paraprofessional helps offset the personal ties of yesterday's well-meaning, but less sophisticated, confidant.

Today's person with problems comes to the paraprofessional for the answer. He expects to be able to explain the way he feels and have the counselor nod and mutter wisely: "Ah, yes, what you have is a well-known complex with a long name and I have the solution. Do exactly as I say and the whole problem will go away." It doesn't work that way. As a matter of fact, the client will not even get outright sympathy from the counselor. But he will get much more. He will get help in working his way through his problem in a logical way. His counselor will help him evaluate how he has overcome similar crises in the past. His counselor will help him sort out the alternatives open to him and explore the consequences of each.

The help he will get will be much more valuable than the kind of help he thought he was going to get. He thought his inner resources had failed him and that the answer could only come from someone else, but he will find out that he is capable of raising himself out of the mental mire that is pulling him down. By mastering the dilemma with his own resources, he grows in the process and strengthens himself for his next problem.

What happens to make a person turn to a hotline or walk-in center? For some reason he can no longer wrestle with his problems single-handedly. The "Anxiety Overheat" light is flashing on his control panel. It flashes brighter and brighter, reminding him that he is out of control. Anxiety, dread and fear are feeding on themselves. The more his tension soars, the more inadequate he feels, and the cycle continues at a maddening rate. His problem might have come on suddenly, like the death of a family member that day, or it might be a problem that has existed for many years but has recently built up to a crisis level. But in either case, there is a temporary overload on his psychological circuitry. Whatever circuit breakers he normally uses to preserve his well-being are not working for him this time, and he needs an outside source of assistance to get his wobbling psyche back in order.

Or to put it another way, he is off balance and he needs a steadying hand for a moment before he can continue on his way. The steadying hand is the external resource that he turns to when his own senses have temporarily failed him.

He won't be in a crisis forever. Sooner or later, in a few hours or a few days at the most, his own system will right itself and pull him out of the tailspin he is in. But he can't wait that long. He wants help now, so he turns to a hotline or counseling center. He thinks that after a talk with the counselor things might be a little better, and they will. The paraprofessional is going to help the client analyze his own system and correct it earlier.

And the encouraging thing about seeking help with a parapro-fessional counselor is that when he pulls out of his psychological nosedive (which he will, in any case, remember), he will do it in the most healthy way for him. He will profit from the mishap by boosting his own self-image and confidence in his own ability to work through his own problems.

Sometimes a client who comes to a paraprofessional has wres-tled with the same problem again and again. Maybe this time the counselor will be able to bring out in him a solution that makes more sense than the ones he has used before. Or maybe this is the first time this problem has ever struck him. That is a beautiful time to get a client because he is going to solve it eventually anyway, and by coming to you for help, he is going to be sorting out his alternatives and putting together his own solution in the most positive and healthy way — from the beginning.

The "Jehovah Complex" with its instant solution for every problem is perhaps the easiest trap for a new counselor. When you come across a person who has all the answers and is anxious to share them at the drop of a problem, keep him away from the hotline or clinic .... or at least from the staff side of the hotline or desk!

The temptation to offer advice is powerful in all of us. We have been giving out advice all of our lives, and many times we should. Very often we owe advice to our family and friends. But the hot-line or counseling service is different, and volunteers or staff aides must learn that difference early on. You *cannot* give advice in a counseling situation. A certain amount of humility is needed in this situation. The counselor must remember that he is, after all, human too. The counselor has his own hang-ups and his own problems. In so many ways he is no better off than the person seeking help.

A solution might seem so simple to the counselor. He might want to blurt out the answer that seems so obvious. But the counselor isn't so smart after all because that client has already heard your solution. His friends have been telling him for a long time that that's what he ought to do. He did not call to get *your* answer (even though he thinks he did or he probably wouldn't have called). What he is really after is *his own solution,* and only his own solution will work for him. Each of us has the key to our own problem. Only we ourselves can unlock that door. How could anybody else ever, ever understand the nuances of our own feelings toward our brother, our teacher, our mistress, or our boss?

If you offer a client your solution to his problem, one of three things will happen, and all three things are bad:

1. He may take your advice and find that your advice doesn't work. You certainly haven't helped him then. He will be even more reluctant to seek outside help next time.

2. He may take your advice and find that it does work. A victory? Not really. When the client was floundering, you proved to him that he could default, throw up his hands, and trust a mental lifeguard to carry him out of his dilemma. You have robbed him of the self-confidence he needs to own up to his own problems. Next time he has a problem, he can just toss it to you or some other counseling center. We learn from dealing with our crises, and we are often stronger humans for having won out over our ordeals. But a gift-wrapped solution can't strengthen us; it can only do the opposite.

3. Or he may not take your advice at all; and, since you have not helped him reach a solution on his own and your interview has led to a solution of your own making which he cannot accept, you have left him back behind where he started. He still has the same problem, no solution of his own, and one less place to turn for help (you).

So we won't offer advice. Another thing we won't offer is sympathy. We have to go against our instincts at this point because we usually do offer sympathy to a person in need or tragedy. But if sympathy could have helped, the client would have turned to friends or any number of convenient places for that.

The following dialogue concentrates on helping the client cope with the situation on his own.

staff aide: Mental Health Center.

client: I hope you can help me.

aide: I'm sure we can. May I have your name, please?

client: What do you need my name for?

aide: We don't have to have your name, but having it makes it easier for us to help you. It makes our conversation easier.

client: Well, my mother gave me one, so you can give me another.

aide: May I call you Mary?

client: Yes, that's a pretty nice name.

aide: Do you live in this area, Mary?

client: Yes, I live near the city park.

aide: How old are you?

client: Twenty-four.

aide: Married?

client: No, I'm not married. Never even came close to it.

aide: Do you have any children?

client: No, I thought about adopting one, but I can't even take care of myself, it seems.

aide: Are you employed?

client: Yes.

aide: Could you tell me what kind of work you do?

client: I don't want my boss involved so do I have to tell you that? I said I'm employed.

aide: No, you don't have to tell us anything you don't want to tell us. We'll just work with the information you feel comfortable giving us. Have you gone to school?

client: Yes, I graduated and had two years of business college.

aide: How did you hear about us?

client: I read the personal column. You folks are near the obituary notices. Gee, what a place for you to be!

aide: Well, we don't have much to say about where they place our ads.

client: I thought it was kind of funny.

aide: Tell me, Mary, I don't have the telephone number you

are calling from; and in case we were disconnected, I
have no way of getting back in touch with you. Would
you give me your phone number please?

client: Yeah, but don't use it. Don't ever call my number
unless I tell you to. Okay?

aide: All right.

client: 448-9861.

aide: And now tell me something, Mary. Are you under any
medication or seeing a physician?

client: No, I wouldn't call it medication. It isn't prescribed.

aide: Would you like to tell me what you mean by that?

client: Well, I take a few pills every now and then.

aide: What kind of pills?

client: Well, sometimes it's red and sometimes it's white.
That's not my problem. I'm all right. I'm not an
addict.

aide: What happened most recently that made you call us?

client: Last night I was watching a movie and that girl, what
she was going through and how she ended up, was so
much like me that it frightened me. I thought I'd better
call and that's why I called.

aide: Well, I don't know the movie that you're speaking
about. Can you tell me something about it? How did it
affect you? And what was it you saw in the movie that
made you feel so upset?

client: Well, this girl didn't have too much of a life or too
much of a connection, you know. She just more or less
did what people taught her. Even what her parents
wanted her to do, she did. She wanted to be a teacher
and her parents thought business school would be the
thing for her. And then that girl just kept everything in
and didn't say too much. And she ended up killing
someone.

aide: Did you feel that you might end up killing someone?

client: I don't know. It's just that when I looked at that girl
and her life, it was so much like mine and I'm just
wondering ....

aide: If you feel like killing someone, do you have any idea who it might be that you would want to kill?

client: I think it would be my boss. He's an old ogre, and he has some of the girls around here crying. He doesn't have me crying. I wouldn't even give him the pleasure of that — seeing me cry.

aide: Why would you want to kill him? What did he do?

client: He thinks he's Casanova, and I'm just waiting for him to tell me that if I don't go to bed with him, I'll lose my job. Those stupid girls, some of them do, you know. I mean, younger cats you can understand; but these old cats, old enough to be your grandfather, I think it's just ridiculous.

aide: Do you have a plan for killing your boss?

client: Well, I'd use a gun. I have one here for my own protection. I'd use a gun, but I haven't got any more of a plan than that. When I saw this thing in the movies, it just got me uptight. I got to thinking, I don't want to go around hurting anyone. I'm telling you, that girl could have been me!

aide: Then if I understand correctly, your problem is that your boss has made your position very uncomfortable for you and, in fact, has angered you so much that you have very strong feelings.

client: Yes, it's the thing I feel inside of me. I just mentioned that because the girl had the same kind of life situation that I have. It's the fear of something in me, the fear that maybe this could happen to me. And this is the thing I'm frightened of. This thing within me ....

CHAPTER THREE

THE ABC METHOD IS THE KEY

THIS book is about the ABC Method or paraprofessional counseling. The Method is a roadmap that will tell the staff aide where he's going in a client interview. The map marks where he is beginning and where he intends to wind up and charts each step along the way.

With the Method the paraprofessional has confidence that he won't get lost or confused along the way. It gives him the confidence he needs to stay in control and be the source of strength that the client so desperately needs.

The Method is an *all-purpose map*. It applies no matter what the client's problem is (except in an emergency where physical help is needed and minutes and seconds are critical). It is a map worked out over a period of time and proven through hundreds of thousands of counseling interviews — both telephone and face-to-face.

The "A, B, C's" of the ABC Method are:

A. *Acquiring*
B. *Boiling Down*
C. *Coping*

Briefly here is what they mean:

In Step A the counselor *acquires* information and rapport. He needs both of them before he can be of any real help to the client.

In Step B he *boils down* the information he has acquired to a well-focused sentence, such as "So really your problem is that you are so preoccupied with your girl friend's rejection that you may flunk out of college, is that it?"

In Step C the counselor begins to help the client *cope* with his problem. He does this by reviewing what alternatives the client has open to him and helping the client commit himself to the alternative that makes the most sense to the client.

Sound easy? It is. Don't think that just because it is simple, it isn't scientific. Don't think that it is an abbreviated or "next-best-thing" method. The psychiatrists who reduced the whole mystical process to the A, B, C steps simply took out all the eight-syllable words and lofty theories and analyzed what steps they themselves were using in their own professional counseling.

There is the Method as simple as the A, B, C in its name. We will use the rest of the book to show how the same method is applied to every kind of problem from suicidal to first love. We'll explore some of the reasoning that underlines the Method, and we'll explore a number of conversations in actual cases that help demonstrate how the Method works in all types of counseling encounters.

When a client calls or visits for help, it's necessary to relieve the anxiety level of two people. One is the client, of course, and the other is the counselor. Actually, at the beginning of the interview, the anxiety of the counselor is more important than the client's. Unless the counselor is calm and thinking clearly, the entire session will be wasted.

So the first part of the ABC Method serves to reduce the tension of both parties. Regardless of how much training a staff aide has, he is going to start off his first few calls with a lot of apprehension. It happens to everyone. When I took my first telephone call after we set up our hotline at the Pasadena, California, Mental Health Center, I was so nervous that I had to excuse myself from the caller to get a drink of water; and I had been helping clients with chronic problems in all phases of social work for twelve years!

We relieve the tension in Step A — the *acquiring* stage. We make it a point not to get into the person's problem too soon. We'll spend the first part of the call or interview finding out a little bit about the client. The information that we acquire will be invaluable to us later when we begin to put the client's problem into the perspective from which he views it. We're not stalling or whiling away the time when we are acquiring; we're accumulating information that we must have. And while we acquire information, we're also acquiring rapport. As the counselor is getting to know the client, the client is getting to know the counselor, and that is terribly important too. The more he can trust his counselor, the more honest and straightforward he'll be about his problem.

During the *acquiring* stage the counselor asks a few specific questions. He needs to know the age of his client, whether he's married and whether he's on medication — prescribed or otherwise. Those pieces of information are going to provide points of reference for the problem. Those answers will help make the counselor better understand what influences the client in his current dilemma.

But just as important as the answers to the prescribed questions, the counselor will be listening for any nonverbal hints he can pick up as well. Clues are everywhere! The client's breathing rate, state of anxiety, pauses, crying, coughing, and sighs are all pieces of nonverbal communication. Even the background noise is a clue. When the client answers, "What do you mean, am I a student? Am I a student!!!", he's telling you something, just as he is when he answers, "Am I married? Well, I'm married and I'm not married." The counselor learns to trust his intuition and pursue these voice inflections and giveaway pauses. He pursues them gently, finding out just what the client meant by those telltale clues he dropped along the way.

The *acquiring* stage will take only a few minutes; but at the end of that brief time, the counselor will have acquired enough background about the client to be able to relate what comes next, and he will have acquired the rapport he needs to explore the problem itself. And what will the client have gotten from it? The client will get the unmistakable feeling that the counselor is trained and is systematic in his approach. He'll now trust the counselor more since his rapport with the counselor has built up too.

The *acquiring* stage gives way to the *boiling down* stage or Step B in the ABC Method. In this step the counselor boils down the things that are disturbing the client until he has boiled them down to a one-sentence description of the problem. "What's such a big deal about that?" someone might ask. "That doesn't sound hard. If you want to know his problem, just ask him. After all, he must have had a specific problem in mind or he wouldn't have called." As logical as that might sound, it just does not work that way. At least not usually. The client is disturbed about the way things are going, but usually he hasn't honestly analyzed his dilemma to sort out the parts. What he will unload on the staff aide will be a jumble of seemingly unrelated thoughts. He'll often bring a whole cast of characters into his drama, and the scenario can be pretty hard to follow sometimes. The reason it all sounds so confusing to the counselor is because the client isn't being honest with himself. He is complicating and obscuring his problem — either intentionally or unintentionally — to keep it from closing in on him.

At this point, the counselor is about to perform the first bit of real service to the client: He's going to help the client disassemble the time bomb he's been living with and lay out all the parts. Then he's going to help pick out the factor that really makes it a problem. The client is going to discover that he has one of three kinds of problems: (1) mental ("I must be going nuts"), (2) interpersonal ("My wife .... ," "My boss .... ," "My teacher .... ," "People .... "), (3) physical ("It began when I got this pain ....").

The *boiling down* stage will reveal whether the client is truly in crisis or is a chronic complainer. The ABC Method is a crisis method for the here and now. It is not a conversation ball to be bounced back and forth with someone who makes a hobby of griping. The *boiling down* stage will determine if the problem is a crisis by finding out what the precipitating stress was and what triggered it.

By the end of the *boiling down* stage, the counselor will know how the client sees his problem (mental, interpersonal or physical) and what the precipitating stress was that caused him to seek help today. Armed with those two clues, he has a handle on what kind of problem is confronting his client; and he can lead the interview into Step C, the *coping* stage.

This is the part that the client came in for in the first place. Steps A and B, *Acquiring* and *Boiling Down*, simply helped the client ask the right questions. Now he'll begin to answer it with Step C, the *Coping* stage.

The most important aid in helping the client cope with his problem is to find out what he's done about the problem when it has come up before. "What did you do about these feelings when you got them before?" "What helped most when this happened before?" "Would the same thing work again, do you think?"

Or if this is the first time the client has faced this particular problem, the counselor still will not offer a solution. "What do you think might work to solve this?" "What else do you think might work?" "Any other solutions that you think might work?" Often the answer to the client's problem may come as the answer to "When you came here tonight to talk to me (or "When you called here today . . . ."), how did you think we might help you?" If the client says, "I don't know," then he should be asked, "If you had a friend who had this same problem, what would you advise him to do?" Or if even that fails, the counselor may ask, "If you had a magic wand that would allow you to solve this problem in any way you wanted, what would you make it do?" It is important for the counselor to show support during this stage because the client is being asked to make some painful and difficult assessments. Consider the following conversation:

client: (child's voice): I am left here all alone and I just don't know what to do.

aide: Where are you?

client: I'm at home and I'm all alone.

aide: Who is usually with you?

client: My mother, but she goes to work every day.

aide: Where is she today?

client: She's at work.

aide: What do you usually do when your mother goes to work?

client: I sit here alone.

aide: I see. The reason you called us today was that you're home alone; and although your mother usually goes to work and you're left home alone, something happened today that made you feel you don't like being alone. Is that right?

client: Yes.

aide: Okay. Has it happened before that you were left alone and didn't like being left alone?

client: Yes. All the time.

aide: So what do you do?

client: I call my grandmother.

aide: Why isn't that working now?

client: My grandmother isn't home.

aide: I see. So why did you call us?
client: Well, I wanted to talk to somebody.

A IS FOR ACQUIRING

IT all starts with *Acquiring*. From the moment the caller speaks or the client comes into view, the counselor begins to acquire information about him. And from the moment the counselor answers, the relationship begins to acquire rapport.

The relationship is between human beings. Both have feelings, biases, and personality traits. The counselor's steady, reassuring manner is adjusted to the situation. He draws upon his natural empathy and understanding to acquire rapport with the client and to acquire information about him. The result will be a "human contact", a very personal approach to helping a fellow human in need.

Both parties begin the relationship with anxiety, so the first part of the interview should be used to overcome the anxiety of both. Don't be nervous. I know that's easy to say and hard to obey; but if you're a listener on a hotline, it will help you to remember that it is impossible to hurt the client during these early minutes. The caller's instinctive psychological shell will keep you from hurting him because at this point you're only a voice to him, not a human relationship. And whether the counseling is by phone or in person, your anxiety should be relieved if you'll remember several things.

In the first place, you're not going to have to come up with some Solomon-like decision and solve the client's problem. The client already has the answer as soon as you meet him; all you'll be doing is helping him discover it himself.

Secondly, you can take solace in the fact that you know the ABC Method and understand how it works. You are beginning on an unknown journey, and you'll be dealing with a problem that will be different from any you've ever dealt with before. But isn't it comforting to know that you already have the map and that the map cannot fail you? You know where you're headed and you know the signposts along the way, so proceed with confidence.

Thirdly, you're going to start slowly and build up to the problem itself. You'll have plenty of chance to catch your breath along the way.

You'll begin the interview by acquiring "identifying information." This information should be on a form in front of you for easy reference and should include the following questions:

Name?

Phone Number?

Have you ever called before?

Age?

Do you live in this area?

Are you a student?

Are you working?

Are you living at home?

Do you have brothers and sisters?

Are you on medication? (prescribed or otherwise)

Have you had any help with your problem?

Keep control of the conversation from the beginning. On a hotline you'll probably begin with something like:

aide: Eastside Hotline.

client: I called to get some advice.

aide: Before we get into your problem, there are a few questions, I'd like to ask you.

Notice that the counselor didn't say, "May I ask you some questions?" The caller may answer "NO!" Do not give him a choice. Say politely, but firmly, that you need to ask a few questions before you go further. You might think that most people would resist giving out all this personal information right off the bat, but experience has proven this just isn't so. People are calling for help. They are prepared to follow your lead because you represent a tower of strength that they have sought.

A few will question you though.

aide: Hello, Lifeline.

client: Yeah, can I talk to somebody about a problem?

aide: I can help you. Before we get into your problem, there are

> a few questions I'd like to ask you. May I have your name?

client: Yeah, I guess so. It's Roger.

aide: And could I have your phone number, Roger?

client: No, why do you want that?

aide: In case we get disconnected for some reason, I'd like to be able to call you back.

client: I still don't want to give it out.

aide: Okay, Roger, if we get disconnected, will you call me back?

The phone number is important, especially in drug overdose, suicidal and homicidal calls. If the interview takes an alarming turn, you'd like to be able to get back to the client. The phrase "in case we get disconnected" may satisfy the client; but if he continues to resist, you can't push it.

Sometimes you don't even get that far, though.

aide: May I have your name?

client: Why do you want to know my name? I thought this was supposed to be an anonymous service.

aide: I need to know a few things about you so I'll be able to help you when we get into your problem.

client: I can't give you my name.

aide: I'd just like to be able to call you by your first name while we're talking.

client: I don't want to give you my name.

aide: Well, I need to call you something. I'll just call you Mary, then.

The counselor should use some name with the client, even if he has to assign him a name. Names will make the interview more personal. It will be a big help in acquiring rapport. If the client balks at giving his name, naturally you don't want to turn right around and aggravate him by asking his phone number. Follow your intuition and use common sense. If the client is hesitant about answering your questions, reassure him with something like, "Be assured we are here to help you, and I want to hear about your difficulty. But first I'd like some information about you so I can be of more help."

Usually when a caller refuses to give his name and phone

number, he is a professional person of some kind. For example, teachers are often reluctant to reveal their names because they fear that it could become part of some file that might be discovered by the Board of Education and threaten their job.

The staff aide can assure the client that the center will make no attempt to contact him without his permission. He need not worry about his family receiving a call from the hotline while he's away and giving away the fact that he's been calling there for help.

The staff aide will acquire the information more or less routinely. Questions will generally bring answers. But that is only half of the *acquiring* stage. The aide must be acquiring rapport at the same time. Acquiring rapport may come easily or it may not. Some clients will trust the staff aide almost immediately. They'll be anxious to talk and spill out their story from the moment they begin to talk. With that kind of client, rapport is acquired very early in the conversation — long before all the information has been acquired.

On the other hand there are clients who want help but are afraid to trust another person. From the beginning of the conversation, the withdrawn client will be morose, elusive or reluctant to talk. If the client is a schizophrenic who has little capacity for human contact, the *acquiring* stage may be very prolonged. In fact, the *acquiring* stage may total 90 percent of the total interview.

Remember, you cannot move on to Step B, the *boiling down* stage, until you have acquired rapport. It is possible for an experienced aide to go on to the *boiling down* stage before he has finished acquiring information because he will be able to weave these questions in as he proceeds. After all, part of the purpose of acquiring information is to relieve the anxiety of the counselor as well as the client. As the counselor becomes more seasoned, he will hear more nuances, more subtle inflections, and more nonverbal hints early in the conversation. His intuition will be more sharply tuned to receive more of what the client is communicating. Then he won't need the steadying device of the initial acquiring of information. He can proceed as soon as he has acquired rapport.

But don't try to short cut the information acquiring before

you've had enough experience. If the client blurts out his problem right away, it's a letdown if you have to back up and ask for simple questions at that point. For example:

aide: Good morning, Community Hotline.
client: Good morning, I'd like to talk over a problem.
aide: Tell me about your problem.
client: I want to kill my wife.
aide: ....

If the staff aide isn't ready to respond quickly and intelligently to that kind of answer, it is awkward (to say the least) to then glance at his form and ask the client how old he is (or worse yet if he is married!).

Actually, the acquiring of information and rapport will continue throughout the interview. But in Step A a basic core of information will be acquired, and an unmistakable rapport must be acquired too. The rapport may start to slip away later because, after all, the exchange is not between two machines but between two human beings .... two personalities. Chances are that the rapport will continue to build as the interview or series of interviews continue(s).

Each counselor's technique and wording will vary since each is a different person, and that's a great thing about the ABC Method. It is not a carefully worded formula of magical words that must be muttered exactly the same way each time to have any effect, but rather it is a general formula that has plenty of room in it for each of our own personalities and warmth. We will all use our own intuition and our own empathy and our own honest way of saying things. The client will recognize that personal integrity through his own intuition. Otherwise, as the ensuing dialogue illustrates, the staff aide and client would never really be able to complete Step A.

aide: Mental Health Center. Can I have your name, please?
client: I will give you my name, but I might as well tell you though, it's not my real name. I'm Maureen Lewis.
aide: Do you live in this area, Maureen?
client: Yes, I live here in the city.
aide: Can I have your phone number, just in case we're

disconnected?

client: I don't believe I want to give you my number this morning. Maybe later, but I'd rather not now.

aide: Okay. How old are you?

client: Eighteen.

aide: Are you married?

client: Yes. I was married. You might say I'm married, I suppose so.

aide: What do you mean by that?

client: My husband and I are getting a divorce, but it looks as though he may want to call it off.

aide: You want to be reconciled? Is that what you're saying?

client: No, he does.

aide: Okay. Do you have any children?

client: Yes, I have one little girl.

aide: How old is she?

client: She's three years old.

aide: Are you working?

client: Yes, I am.

aide: What is your income?

client: It varies. Sometimes it's pretty high and sometimes not so much. Most of the time I make a pretty good income.

aide: What is your job?

client: Do I have to tell you? Well, maybe I'd better tell you because it does have a bearing on the problem. I hate to tell you. I don't want to shock you.

aide: No, whatever you tell us is confidential.

client: It won't shock you?

aide: No.

client: Well, I'm a hustler. Well, you want to really know, I work with men. I'm a prostitute. We prefer to call ourselves hustlers.

aide: How did you hear about our Center?

client: Well, you have a radio program, and there are ads in magazines every now and then. I've been reading them and listening to the radio, and I really do have a problem I'd like to discuss with you.

CHAPTER FIVE

B IS FOR BOILING DOWN

N OW that we know something about the client, we are going to have to work to find out what his problem actually is.

"Ridiculous!" you mutter.

"Backwards!" you add.

And it is true that this sounds like a system invented to complicate — rather than simplify — the counseling process. Not only did we take care not to ask about the problem at the beginning of the interview, but we are now prepared for difficulty in finding out what the problem really is. It does sound like a backwards way of going about things.

But the ABC Method is logical and it is simple. And it really is difficult to find out what the problem is, believe it or not. Oh sure, the client came to you because he was uptight and had "had it up to here"; but strangely enough, people quite often don't admit their real problems to themselves. Whether we like to admit that or not, it's true of most of us.

The second stage in the ABC Method is the *Boiling Down* stage. We're going to boil down the rambling and the emotion to the real problem bothering our client. The client himself may be surprised to isolate the exact problem.

During the *boiling down* stage be prepared for a lot of words, a lot of rambling, and a lot of detours. The client isn't playing tricks with you, he's playing tricks with himself. Not wanting to admit his real problem to himself, he camouflages it with pseudo-problems and pseudo-gripes. During this second stage, the para-professional counselor painstakingly stalks the true problem, brushing away the foliage that might get in the way, until he is able to say: "Then if _____ were taken care of, there wouldn't be a problem, is that right?" When the client can confirm the counselor's definition of the problem, the counselor is half way home.

During the second stage the counselor encourages the client to

28

talk, but not to ramble. The counselor skillfully directs the client's conversation through the right questions. The client may not be going anyplace in particular, but the counselor is.

The counselor needs to know two things to confirm the exact problem.

First, the counselor needs to know what type of problem it is and, secondly, what brought it on.

There are only three types of problems that clients will bring you because all of the problems we have as mortal human beings fall into these three categories: (1) mental, (2) interpersonal, or (3) physical. What brought on that problem was a precipitating stress. Let's take the type of problem first.

The mental problem is one that is within us. It is caused by our own anxiety and depression. "I can't cope," "I must be going nuts," are comments typical of clients with mental problems.

The interpersonal problem is a problem with other people; "My wife is rotten . . . .", "My lover rejects me . . . .". These are all the beginnings of statements about interpersonal problems.

The physical problem is basically a medical problem. "I hurt physically," the client is saying. "This pain in my head is driving me crazy . . . .". Only a doctor can help this client. No amount of counseling will do any good. "If only my leg would quit hurting me . . . ." is a complaint from the physical problem.

Remember, the problem of the client is one of three: mental, interpersonal or physical. He may describe many different problems or a terribly complex one. But he called about one specific problem and that is the one the counselor is going to concentrate on, as soon as he can isolate it. The counselor will generally brush aside the other problems and deal only with the one that caused the client to call or stop in. That one problem is the one that the client can't cope with at the moment. Obviously, if a secondary problem is suicidal or homicidal, the counselor will want to protect the client and others by dealing with that problem too; but, normally, the counselor's concern is the client's single, preoccupying problem of the moment.

To get at the type of problem bugging the client, the counselor begins by determining the precipitating stress. What (specifically) brought this problem on.

There are three kinds of precipitating stresses that could have caused the client to call: (1) loss of control, (2) loss of dependency, or (3) a new adjustment or change in the client's life situation. The counselor finds out what the precipitating stress was:

aide: What made you call tonight?

client: My roommate has been strung out on drugs since we started rooming together last year.

aide: But what happened tonight that made you call?

client: Things have just been building up for the last few weeks till I had to talk to someone about it.

aide: But why tonight? What was it that happened tonight that made you decide to call this number and talk to us about it?

client: Well, my roommate came in this afternoon and started "throwing hands." He knocked me around pretty bad.

aide: Has he fought with you before?

client: No. He's come home pretty high before, but it never came to violence.

In the above case the counselor was not satisfied until he had isolated the precipitating stress. Although the caller said he was calling because of a long term problem, the counselor knew something specific had triggered the phone call. Now the counselor knows the precipitating stress. The client lost control of the roommate situation today.

From here, the counselor will get the client to talk about his feelings towards the roommate. The type of problem still isn't known.

> [It could be mental] Something must be wrong with me. I'm on the same drugs he is and I can't get off the stuff. [Or it could be interpersonal] I can't get along with him, and I don't think I can make it until the end of the semester with this bum, [Or again, it could be physical] Ever since he hit me in the stomach, I've felt like something was hurt badly inside me, but if I go to the doctor ....

The conversation may wander quite a bit during the second stage, and it may become frustrating to the counselor when it seems to be going nowhere. But through it all, the counselor must pin the rambling back to the real problem. He must *boil down* what is said to arrive at the real problem. The counselor becomes a detective as he sifts through the words looking for clues.

When the counselor thinks he has the problem, he summarizes it in a sentence to see if the client agrees: "So the problem that made you call tonight is that you're running a physical risk by staying with your roommate and you may get hurt again. Is that right?" If the client doesn't think that sums up his problem, the search continues.

Sooner or later though, the client and the counselor will agree on a one-sentence definition of the real problem. At this point the counselor can say something like: "So if the dean would assign you to another dorm, that would solve the problem. Is that right?" If the client agrees that this would be a solution, the second phase is concluded and the counselor escorts the client into the third phase of the ABC Method — C for *Coping*.

aide: What happened today that made you call us, Mrs. Green?

client: I feel like I want to end it all. I can't think anymore, I just can't.

aide: WHAT IS IT THAT HAPPENED TODAY?

client: My husband left me. He left me with eight kids. He's done that two times before, but this time he said he really means it. I can't raise these kids by myself — eight kids.

aide: Mrs. Green, you say he did this two times before?

client: Yes, he did.

aide: And what happened those two other times?

client: Well, I tell you I went and I begged him to come back, and I lied and told him I was pregnant, and he came back. Then the next time the police brought him back; they were going to put him in jail so he decided to come home. I just can't stand this anymore.

aide: Why?

client: Oh, I just feel like I want to end it here. I feel like what's the use? I can't let this thing go on. I blame myself. It's something I'm doing that's causing him to leave.

aide: What do you think you're doing?

client: I don't know. I'm just not a good wife or a good mother or something. I don't know. Something's wrong.

aide: When he left the other two times, did you feel it was your fault?

client: Yes, I do. I told him to leave. I told him he wasn't any good and he ought to leave, and so he left.

aide: Why did you tell him that?

client: I was hoping we could move into a better house. This neighborhood isn't the best. And then I wanted him to get another job. He was working two jobs, and I just thought he needed to get another job. He told me *I* needed to look for something because he was tired, and I told him I had to raise the kids, y'know how it goes. And then the little boy, he broke his leg; everything piled up. And then the bill collectors, you know how it goes. So it was really my fault; I just nagged him to death.

aide: Did you do this each time when he came back again?

client: Yes, you see because it's just that things don't change. We don't do things together; he's too tired, and I guess I just ought to be more understanding. But I'd like to get away from the kids sometimes; but he comes home, watches the TV and goes to sleep; and I'm left with everything, it seems.

aide: Have you ever told him this?

client: Well, I scream when I tell him, and it's always arguing instead of sitting down rationally. I used to be a rational person when I was in high school.

aide: Let's go back a little bit. You feel you nagged him too much.

client: Yes, that's what he tells me. He tells me I really don't want him and I really don't need him, and so he says it's better he should leave me and the kids and I'd be happy without him. But that's not true.

aide: You want him?

client: Yes, I do, I really do.

aide: Did you tell him that?

client: I tell him after he leaves.

aide: Do you ever tell him your feelings for him?

client: Well, not really, I just think he ought to know. He ought to understand. After all, I'm his wife.

aide: Do you think he wants to be with you?

client: I don't think he has time for other women. I'm not concerned about that either because as long as he uses discretion, it's all right with me. But I don't know, I guess I want too much. I wanted eight kids, and I got eight kids; and he says that's what I wanted and everything I want I get, he says. But he said he can't do it any longer, it's too much.

aide: Do you feel you gave him everything he wanted?

client: No, not really, I really don't.

aide: What is it you want that you aren't getting?

client: That's why I think something's wrong with me. It seems as if something's wrong with me that makes me act like this.

aide: How do you want to deal with this? What do you want to do about it?

client: I'd like to get some help. I can't go on like this. My kids are going to be all messed up if I continue. I really want my husband back, but the same thing happens over and over. That's not right. I have to start getting some kind of help.

aide: Did you have any kind of help the other two times?

client: Well, my mother, she flew in. You know mothers. Boy, that mother of mine, she's something. She just said, you folks have got to get together with all those kids to take care of, and so he came back. Then the last time I talked to a friend. But your friends get tired of that. But that's what helped the last time. So I think if I could get someone to talk to, but not my friends or my mother.

aide: Well, who would you like to talk to?

client: I really think there's something wrong with me, and I think I need to talk to someone who knows how to work with people when there's something wrong with them.

CHAPTER SIX

C IS FOR COPING

WE have come a long way by now. Chances are the session is well over halfway completed; and so far we haven't even begun to talk about solutions, even though the client called or stopped in for a solution.

It's a little bit like the huge factory that ground to a halt one day with thousands of workers standing idly by as the engineers tried in vain to fix the machinery. A mechanical genius was summoned from a downtown consulting firm. The mechanical wizard jogged along the lines, the wheels and levers, looking up and down, until he suddenly stopped, whipped out a screwdriver and tightened a single screw. The machinery moved again, the workers took up their places, and the problem solver produced an invoice for a thousand dollars for tightening the single screw. The plant's management gladly paid the bill, knowing that the solution was simple, but that determining the problem had taken true expertise.

Sometimes the solution to a personal crisis is easy and sometimes it is not so easy; but before we can begin to think about the solution, we have to be sure we know precisely what problem we are trying to solve.

During the A stage or first stage, we *Acquired* the background we would need to understand the problem. During the B stage or second stage, we *Boiled Down* the facts to isolate the problem. During the C stage we can begin to help the client *Cope* with the problem we have just isolated.

The C stage is difficult for the counselor because of the human tendency to offer a solution to the client. But the counselor must bite his tongue, take a pledge, hang a plaque on the wall, and promise himself faithfully not to offer advice to the client. Never give advice (except in suicidal and homicidal cases). It is the client who must cope .... not the counselor. It is the client's problem .... not the counselor's. It is the client who can best sort out the alternatives that will work for him .... not the counselor. Your mission is to help the client find his own solution. You are as mortal as he is. You are not omnipotent or omniscient, all-powerful or all-knowing. You are not Jehovah or any other deity. You must be humble and remember your mortal status, even though the client probably will not.

The client's problem is not lack of advice. He's gotten advice from all directions. And he's heard the solution you would probably offer many times before. You don't tell an alcoholic that his solution is to quit drinking. Don't you think he's thought of that? Don't you think his family and friends might have offered that solution?

But if it is true that one shouldn't offer advice, it is just as true that you can't cop out by simply tossing the ball back to the client and saying, "It's your problem, you figure out the solution."

The C or *Coping* stage involves a few techniques, just like the other stages. The *coping* stage technique is to explore with the client the alternatives that have worked for him before and alternatives that might work for him in this case.

The counselor will achieve three things during this stage of the interview: (1) he will develop the client's problem-solving potential by guiding his conversation; (2) he will help the client inventory how he has coped with similar problems in the past and what alternatives are open to him at the present; and (3) he will leave the client with a plan of action, arrived at through a goal-setting process. The key words are (1) problem-solving, (2) inventory and (3) goal setting.

You begin by exploring the problem-solving ability of the client. How has he coped in times past? If the problem is a recurring one, you must find out what has worked in previous episodes. You ask, "How did you handle this problem when it came up before?" Or "What did you try the other times when this came up?"

Or if this is a first time for this particular problem, try to explore what the client has done in similar cases. "Has anything of a similar nature happened to you before that you could compare this to? Were there any experiences from that instance that might provide some solutions in this case?"

It is often very helpful to a client to be directed in this way. You are forcing him to explore his own problem-solving resources and his own alternative solutions. If the solution proposed by the client is clearly unworkable, then ask about other solutions. If, for example, a client's solution to the present problem is suicide and the solution in times past was to seriously consider suicide, ask what other alternatives are open. "Apart from suicide what other solutions are there that might help in this situation?" you might ask.

Next, have the client inventory the courses of action open to him. Encourage the client to use his imagination to add to the list of possible alternatives. Obviously, the wider the choice of selections, the better able the client will be to choose the very best solution for him. Although the inventory process seems simple to you as you encourage the client to think of the alternatives open to him, remember that *your* circuits are clear .... you are not in a period of emotional overload.

The client is threatened with extreme mental vertigo or loss of balance at the time of the call or interview. That loss of balance is short-circuiting his normal, rational thought process. You must walk him logically through the alternatives open to him, exploring each in a logical, objective, reasoned way. It is as if you are talking by short wave radio to a downed pilot in the wilderness whose life is threatened by the extreme cold. You can't hand him a blanket over the radio. You have got to think — through his eyes and his perception — of the kinds of tools he has at his disposal around him. Using his knowledge of his immediate surroundings and your calm objectivity, you have to inventory the things he has access to that could provide solutions.

The inventory must come from the client or the interview is stalemated. Even if the client develops a mental block and can't come up with any possible courses of action, you are providing no help at all to draw up the list for him.

If the client can't think of any solutions, you may have to ask him to think it over and call back or come back in. Tell him to "sleep on it" and give it some more thought. Tell him you'll think about it some more, too. But don't proceed until the client arrives at a solution or solutions which he thinks will have a bearing on the present problem.

aide: So the real problem, Susan, is that you're considering running away because your parents leave you alone to take care of your sister; and you don't consider that fair since your sister is only six and as a fifteen-year old, you've got a life of your own to lead. Does that sum up the problem pretty well?

client: Yeah, I guess that's it. You hit the nail on the head.

aide: Or let's look at it another way. If you had more time for yourself and your parents didn't make you take care of your baby sister so much, would you still have problems that were big enough to make you think about leaving home?

client: No.

aide: We've talked about an awful lot tonight, and you've mentioned quite a few problems, but it looks like we've boiled it all down to the key problem now.

client: Yeah, if my parents didn't saddle me with my sister all the time and I had more time for what I want to do, that would solve everything.

aide: You say this has been going on for a long time. Let's go back and see when it began. How old were you then?

client: I guess when I was about ten.

aide: Your parents started leaving you to take care of your sister when you were ten? Then your sister must have been a pretty small baby.

client: Yeah, that's right.

aide: Was there any other time when you felt that this was an injustice?

client: Yeah, there were lots of times.

aide: What did you do in those cases?

client: I just got mad and cried and wished it weren't happening to me.

aide: When you called us tonight, what did you think we could do for you?

client: I thought you could put me in touch with a psychiatrist.

aide: What did you think a psychiatrist could do for you?

client: Oh, I don't know. Maybe he could straighten out my thinking.

aide: Besides seeing a psychiatrist, what else might be a solution for you?

client: I suppose I could talk to my parents about what this was doing to me.

aide: Have you tried that before?

client: No, I never let them know what this was doing to me. I was too proud, I guess. It sounds kind of silly, but I never really talked to them about how much this was hurting me.

CHAPTER SEVEN

IT ALL COMES TOGETHER HERE

THE counselor is going to do his best to send the client on his way or conclude the interview with a definite plan of action for the client. Thus, the client is getting the solution he came in for. But the solution will not have come from the paraprofessional counselor, as the client expected, but from a most unexpected source .... himself.

It is exasperating in many cases to witness a client struggle with a decision that seems so simple from the other side of the desk or the other end of the phone. There is that ever-present temptation to step outside the ABC Method and point out the solution to the client. But remember what will happen if the client leaves with the counselor's solution rather than his own.

(1) If he takes your advice and finds it doesn't work, you're nothing but one more friend with a piece of useless advice.

(2) If he takes your advice and it *does* work, you've proved to him that he can't solve his own problems. He'll need another crutch next time.

(3) If he doesn't think your advice is worth taking, then he'll be even more reluctant to seek competent outside help next time.

By now the client has laid out the alternative courses of action open to him and has reviewed the courses of action that have been helpful in the past. He must now narrow down that list to a goal that makes sense to him.

The client may hedge when the time comes to actually make a decision about the course to pursue. But remember how difficult this step is for some people. You're asking the client to walk on his own, using his own inner resources. That won't come easily for the client who isn't used to leaning on himself instead of someone else. Don't give up if he throws up his hands at first.

Help the client along by asking how he thought your service could help him when he first called or stopped in. After all, he thought you could offer some kind of solution or he wouldn't have leaned on you to begin with. Turn back to that decision, and you direct him to the kind of solution he was looking for all the time. Gently prod his thinking along these lines. "How did you think I could help you when you called?" "What kind of solution did you think we could offer?"

If that still doesn't work, try this: Ask him what he would advise a friend to do in a similar situation. Don't ask him about a family member because that brings a whole set of subjective feelings into the question. But what would he advise a friend to do with the same problem?

Usually, the advice-to-a-friend method will be enough to get him out of his own shell enough to look at the problem more objectively. But if that doesn't work, there's one more thing you can try.

"How would you solve this problem if you had a magic wand and could do anything with it you wanted?", you could ask. Now you have stretched the client's imagination to the limits. You have removed all of the constraining obstacles that reality has put in his way. He should be free to think about the problem in the abstract now and begin to offer solutions that can be brought back within the bounds of real life.

Multiple solutions must be narrowed down to a single goal. This is done by weighing each alternative. "Why would you choose this approach?", the counselor might ask. "What would happen if you did that?"

Ultimately, the interview ends with a goal .... a plan that the client thinks has some chance of working. The counselor is careful to elicit enough details of the plan from the client to make sure it is a plan that the client can follow through on. A timetable is important for the goal if it is to be put into effect.

And now with a goal agreed upon by the counselor and the client, the interview concludes. The goal is the final product of what may have been a long, frustrating, emotional dialogue. The client is leaving the interview or hanging up from the conversation with a diploma or plan of action that he has earned the hard way. It was the client who laid out the pieces of the puzzle in terms of his background and circumstances. It was the client who described the problem in broad terms and boiled it down to a specific, identifiable problem. It was the client who listed the alternatives and chose the most logical one from among them. And it is the client who is leaving the interview with the resolve to put his own plan into action.

Actually, it could have worked no other way, but the ABC Method has worked with one human being holding the flashlight while a brother or sister found his or her own way. It can be a beautiful feeling for both.

SUICIDE AND HOMICIDE — THE ULTIMATE CRISES

Suicide! Homicide! The very words bring a chill, as well they should. Suicide and murder are the ultimate acts because they bring about the deliberate snuffing out of a precious human life.

Many of the problems brought to a counseling service, telephone or walk-in, deal with suicide and homicide; and it is a tribute to the counseling centers' abilities that these ultimate problems have been dealt with so effectively by paraprofessionals. In fact, it is precisely these crises that have underlined the need for paraprofessional counseling services, and it is the paraprofessionals' record of success that has spurred the growth of paraprofessional services.

To prevent a suicide or homicide is truly to save a life that otherwise might have ended. One of the greatest rewards of paraprofessional counseling is knowing that you were prepared to deal with a life-and-death situation and because of you someone is alive today who might have died had you not been there to help.

Suicide and homicide are the ultimate human problems, all right; but like any other problems brought to a counselor, they are problems that the client wants to overcome. You have a head start already. And there are proven ways of dealing with the suicidal and homicidal client. The paraprofessional is trained and ready for just such emergencies and is equipped with counseling techniques that are based on millions of hours of experience.

"I called you because I'm going to kill myself," says the voice at the other end of the line. You take a deep breath and begin the process of saving the life that may be hanging on by the telephone line and nothing more.

But before looking into the technique of handling suicide calls, let's take a look at suicide itself. Suicide is a threat to every part of

42

society. Suicide candidates are young and old, male and female, married and single, wealthy and poor, white and black. For years the youth ("who had too much to live for") and blacks ("who had too little to die for") were poor candidates for suicide. But the black comedians' joke that "blacks don't commit suicide because you can't jump out of a basement window" doesn't ring true anymore. Suicide among blacks is on the rise, and suicide among youth under the age of twenty-two is now the third leading cause of death.

All in all, some 25,000 suicides occur each year in the United States, and for every successful suicide there are nine unsuccessful attempts by people who may very well try again.

Suicide is still a subject shrouded in mystery and misinformation for most Americans. A number of myths manage to hang on from generation to generation, and these myths cloud many people's thinking about suicide. Here are some of them:

Myth 1: Don't worry about the person who talks about suicide, worry about the one who doesn't. People who talk about suicide don't follow through.
Eight out of ten people who commit suicide clearly announced their intentions.

Myth 2: Suicide tendencies "run in the family." They are inherited.
Not so!

Myth 3: People who attempt suicide (or succeed in it) are possessed with a "death wish" and want to die, so it's useless to try to stop them.
Wrong! Suicidal people generally can't make up their minds and waiver back and forth up to the very end. Even in their decision to attempt suicide, they usually do it in a way that leaves them an "out" with the possibility of a last-minute rescue. In effect, they "gamble with death."

Myth 4: Once suicidal, always suicidal.
Not so. People who are suicidal are only in that condition during a short phase of their lives.

Myth 5: Suicidal people are crazy.
Unhappy, for sure, but not mentally ill in the vast majority of

cases.

Myth 6: Once saved from suicide, a person is cured of the impulse. *Untrue. Out of every five suicides, four were "repeat attempts."*

Myth 7: Most suicides are caused by a sudden, traumatic event. *No. Most suicides follow prolonged periods of dejection and feelings of helplessness or low esteem.*

Myth 8: Suicide victims are mostly women.
Although twice as many women attempt suicide, twice as many men succeed in killing themselves.

The suicidal client presents a complex picture to the counselor. He sounds and acts disorganized, hopeless and helpless. He is confused and reflects a number of feelings including rejection and loneliness. His call or visit to the counseling service is a groping for help, even though the kind of help being sought is not clearly defined.

As soon as the client mentions the possibility of suicide, even in an off-hand or joking way, the aide should instinctively zero in on that possibility. Everything else becomes secondary until the suicidal feelings can be worked through. The first priority for the aide is to determine how serious is the threat. There are a number of indicators that will help in this evaluation.

If there is any possibility that the client has already attempted suicide and is in physical danger, from ingested pills, bleeding wrists, or other causes, the aide is confronted with medical — not mental — emergency. The counseling can and must wait. It's now a matter of saving a life through medical treatment. Get the client's name and phone number, if this hasn't been done already, because you'll want to call back in case you get disconnected. You'll also want to know where to send emergency equipment if needed. If the client won't give you his phone number and is in immediate physical harm, start tracing the number.

If there is no medical emergency, the aide should try to determine how specific the suicidal client's plan is by asking "How do you plan to kill yourself?" *Always use harsh terms for death with the suicidal client, not euphemisms. Use "kill yourself" instead of "do yourself in." Use "death," not "pass away." You're trying for as much shock value as possible now, trying to sober a suicidal person with the ugly, unseemly aspect of what he is contemplating.*

The client will tip his hand as to his seriousness when he answers the question about how he intends to kill himself. If he replies that he hasn't thought that far ahead, the threat is minimal. On the other hand, if the client's plan involves shooting, hanging, drinking poison or driving his car into a freeway piling, his threat must be taken seriously. If he has the plan thought out to such small details as the time and place, which gun he'll use and how, and what will be in the suicide note, the threat is serious indeed.

There are some other generalizations that will help the aide evaluate the seriousness of a suicidal call or visit. Generally, threats from males are more serious than those from females. The older a suicidal person, the greater the threat. The more disoriented the caller sounds, the more seriously the call should be taken. If the client is yelling and belligerent the threat is quite serious.

The ABC Method is short-circuited at whatever point suicide enters the picture. After determining how serious the threat is, the counselor should begin immediately to look for the reason. "Why do you want to kill yourself?", the aide should ask. This should bring the precipitating stress out into the open.

Then the aide should begin to collect alternatives from the client. "What would help solve this problem other than suicide?", the aide should ask; then follow with "Okay, that's one possibility. What else would help solve it?" The client must be forced back out of the box he has worked himself into: concluding that suicide is the answer or a good answer to his problem. The client should be left with a "contact", a jointly-agreed-upon plan of action which the client intends to follow after leaving the phone or the counselor's office.

The aide should assure himself that the client has the resources he needs to get him through the immediate crisis. If the threat of suicide is serious, a relative or friend should stay with the client or spend the night with him. Set an exact time for the next interview and that will give the client something else to live for and something else to preoccupy himself with other than his own death.

And finally, extract a promise that he won't kill himself without calling you back in advance. In this way you are more sure about getting help again for the client if the situation gets worse.

One final word about counseling suicidal people: If you do the very best you can and still the client ends up taking his own life, remember, that person acted on his own. He had a personal choice to make, and he made the ultimate decision. Don't be burdened down with a sense of failure as a paraprofessional counselor. Remember, clients of the most renowned psychiatrists on earth commit suicide too. One must continue the rewarding calling of paraprofessional counseling without keeping a grim tally sheet, but rather with a sense of helping those who can and will help themselves to do so.

Closely related to the problem of suicide is the problem of homicide. Each year some 20,000 lives are violently ended in this country at the hands of another human being; and while the suicide rate in the United States has remained at a fairly constant rate of fifteen to sixteen per 100,000 people sixteen years or older, the homicide rate continues to climb. In 1960 the homicide rate was 7.0 per 100,000; by 1970 it had climbed to 11.0 per 100,000.

The aide should suspect homicidal tendencies when violence shows up in the client's background, and unprovoked hostility and aggression are evident. A background of sex crimes, child molestation, child-battering and assault and battery should signal an aide to probe for homicidal tendencies.

If the counselor suspects homicidal tendencies in a client, he should probe to see if an exaggerated bitterness towards another person carries with it the thought of murder. This is done almost casually by asking, "Have you ever thought about doing serious harm to someone?" If the client responds in the affirmative, he'll usually soften this admission with some sort of qualifier, such as, "Yes, but I'm too chicken to carry it out," or "I wouldn't really go through with it." An aide should then probe a bit farther, along the same lines as with a suicidal client, by finding out how specific the client is about this thought of killing someone else.

The aide should ask, "Have you thought how you would do it?" If the client doesn't have any sort of plan, then there is no real threat. Almost everyone has had thoughts at some time in their lives wishing the untimely departure of someone else. If the client describes a specific plan, though, take the threat seriously. This is one of the few cases where the aide has a responsibility to people other than the client.

Upon learning that the client has developing ideas about homicide, the aide must begin to *acquire* information in a determined direction. As much information as possible must be built up about the client's background leading up to this tendency. What about the job? What about school? What are the client's backgrounds in sex and love and religion and marriage? What's his family life like? How does he spend his time at work and at play? How about his habits? Do they include gambling or drugs or alcohol? Has he had brushes with the law?

Depending on the direction this dialogue takes, the aide either begins to satisfy himself that the threat is more of a thought than a plan of actual murder, or he begins to conclude that there is a very real possibility that a murder will be committed unless something is done about the client's tendencies right away.

If the aide becomes convinced that the threat is minimal, then the interview should continue along the lines of the ABC Method by *acquiring* information about the client and *boiling* it down to the client's real problem. But if the aide becomes convinced that the client is dangerously homicidal, steps must be taken to share that knowledge with the client's family and with civil authorities. The aide should seriously consider hospitalizing the client and insuring psychiatric evaluation. Remember, the fact that the client called or came in to see you about a homicidal or suicidal problem means that the part of him that doesn't want to do it is the strongest — this is what you will be working with. Secondly, this is a true crisis situation; and remember, a crisis is an opportunity for help. Chances are that whatever the two of you agree to the client will follow.

CHAPTER NINE

SUBSTANCE ABUSE: ALCOHOL AND DRUGS MEAN PROBLEMS

WHAT if every man, woman and child in New York City were dead drunk? What if everybody in the suburbs of New York City — in New York State and New Jersey too — were all drunk? That would total a grand sum of nine million drunks! Well, that would still be a million drunks short of the total number of alcoholics in the United States today. The American Medical Association estimates that there are ten million alcoholics in the United States. The greater New York City population is nine million.

Alcoholism is a monumental problem. Compare those ten million alcoholics to the 500,000 drug addicts in the United States, and you find more than twenty alcoholics for every drug addict.

I'm not minimizing the drug problem. I've spent too much of my life working with drug addicts to do that. But I do want to point out that our society has tended to publicize the narcotic and drug problem more than alcohol addiction when really both of them are a part of the same problem in our society: *substance abuse.*

Substance abuse is a problem for society, and it is a problem that has enormous playback through the counseling services. A large percentage of client contacts with counseling services involve a substance abuse problem. Perhaps the abuse or addiction itself is the reason for the client's seeking counseling. Or perhaps substance abuse simply figures into a larger problem. But in either case, the counselor should know something about addiction to understand the client's confrontation with this problem.

There are so many problems brought to the paraprofessional or nondegreed counselor; why a chapter on this specific problem? Why not chapters on divorce and sex and infidelity and so many other common problems? Why are there only two chapters in this book on specific problems? There's a good reason. The chapter on

48

suicide and homicide is important because its life-and-death problems need fast, well-directed help; and that help is sometimes a departure from the ABC Method of counseling which has been stressed throughout the rest of the book. This chapter on alcohol and drugs is important because substance abuse brings an external factor into the client's problem. A client can think out his options and use his mind to work out his own problems in most other cases. But when alcohol or drugs are present, the mind is only partially at the beck and call of the client. He does not have the full use of his own mind, and hence his understanding of his problem and his ability to sort out his options are greatly hampered.

Who is the narcotic addict? About half of the addicts are white and about half are black, with a small percentage left over for other races. Half of the drug addicts in this country are in their twenties and about a fourth of them are in their thirties. The other one-fourth are split between the under-twenty segment and over-forty segment. And while narcotic addicts come from all races and from the well-to-do sector as well as the not-so-well-to-do, statistics show that the vast majority of addicts come from socially deprived backgrounds. As in so many other aspects of life, those families already burdened with the greatest problems are hit worst by the drug problem. A great many addicts have only one parent, and most of them are found to have had a bad relationship with their fathers. They generally fared poorly in school and got into sex and promiscuity long before their peers. They are defiant of authority, often have records of juvenile delinquency and had trouble holding a job even before they took up drugs.

When we talk about the "drug problem," we are really talking about four major types of drugs: (1) alcohol, (2) narcotics, (3) "dangerous drugs" and (4) hallucinogens.

Aside from alcohol, the narcotics family represents the greatest problem to society and to the individuals unlucky enough to get caught in their grip. There are three drugs in the narcotics group: (1) opiates, (2) cocaine and (3) marijuana. By far the most dangerous of these are the opiates, which include morphine, heroin and codeine. Of the 500,000 addicts in the United States, a whopping 90 - 95 percent are hooked on heroin. Because such a large

percentage of drug addicts are hooked on heroin, the counselor
needs to understand how heroin and the other opiates act on an
individual.

The amount of time that an individual takes heroin before
becoming addicted is tragically short. A period of a few weeks is
enough. Almost overnight the victim is dependent on the drug,
and from then on his tolerance level increases so that he needs to
take more and more of the drug just to avoid withdrawal symptoms. Without the drug he develops stomach pains, sweating,
paleness and a feeling of collapse. In the beginning the victim
took the drug for a pleasurable sensation; but all too soon he is
taking the drug not to feel good, but to avoid feeling bad. Obviously as his demand for the drug grows to greater and greater
quantities, it takes more and more money to finance the habit. An
addict's supply of opium or heroin cost him $25 to $150 *a day*, or
$5,000 to $30,000 per year. No wonder the addict must steal and
turn to prostitution for money to sustain the habit! No wonder
other necessities, such as the right kinds of food, are left out of the
budget!

The opium or heroin client is generally non-combative, sexu-
ally impotent, unambitious and without a steady job. His drug
brings him daydreams about wealth and fame . . . . but it does not
bring the corresponding drive to accomplish the dreams. The
opium/heroin client needs only a few weeks (or a few months at
the most) of "cold turkey" abstinence, along with its painful
withdrawal symptoms, to overcome his physical dependence on
the drug. A nominal jail sentence will cure the heroin addict of
the physical addiction; yet the psychological habit is so strong
that virtually 100 percent of the "cold turkey" cures go back on the
habit once they return to the peers and environment that is
"home" to them. Fortunately, the formal programs of narcotic
treatment are much more successful and permanently cure a sub-
stantial percentage of those on their programs.

The other drugs in the narcotic family are cocaine and marijuana. Neither of these are nearly as significant to the crisis counselor as the opiate family of narcotics. Cocaine is a powerful
stimulant, causing the opposite effect from opiates; and cocaine
does not create physical addiction. Marijuana does not cause

physical dependence either. It acts on some people as a stimulant and on others as a depressant, but in either case, its effects wear off after a few hours. Short-term effects might include nausea and vomiting, but marijuana causes no long-term effects and no fatalities from its use have been recorded.

Next, let's look at the so-called "dangerous drugs": amphetamines and barbiturates. Among the stimulants, "pep pills" or amphetamines are the most common and the most abused. Physical addiction does develop with amphetamines and the tolerance level continues to rise with usage. The effects of amphetamines vary from nervousness and insomnia (from a routine dosage) up to wild hallucinations and delusions (from a dosage too extreme for the user's tolerance level). "Bennies" and "Dexies" are the street nicknames for Benzadrine® and Dexadrine®, which are legitimate prescription drugs. Amphetamines are taken orally in their regular pharmaceutical form or injected intravenously in diluted powder form.

The depressant family includes the much-abused barbiturates, which *do* cause physical addiction with overuse. There are twenty-five different barbiturates on the market for medical use. Barbiturates are significant drugs to the counselor because they often lead to crisis situations and suicide. When taken in excess, barbiturates (or "goofballs" as they are known) cause a drunk-like reaction, including slurred speech, staggering walk, tremors, emotional impairment and lapses in judgement. The withdrawal symptoms are extreme. Barbiturate withdrawal can cause delirium convulsions and major psychological crises. They can lead to suicide or accidental death.

Besides narcotics (opiates) and dangerous drugs (stimulants and depressants), there is a third major family of abused drugs, the hallucinogens, also known as the psychedelic drugs. The best known of these hallucinogens is LSD, which is taken in pill form or in liquid form dissolved in sugar cubes. LSD has bizarre effects on its user. Senses of sight, hearing, and taste run together in wild and fantastic forms. The user almost literally goes "out of his mind" as he loses his ego identity and begins to act outside his normal personality, suddenly taking on homosexual impulses or other traits abnormal for that particular user. The user can

COMMON PSYCHOACTIVE DRUGS OF ABUSE*

DRUG CLASS	OTHER NAMES	ACUTE HIGH DOSES	MENTAL TOLERANCE
Narcotics†	heroin, morphine, Demerol,® Talwin,® codeine, Dilaudid,® Methadone,® Darvon,® "hard stuff," "smack"	Kill—often	Yes
Sedatives†	barbiturates, Seconal,® Amytal,® Tuinal,® "rainbows," "reds," "yellows," "downers," Doriden,® Quaalude,® "sopers"	Kill—often	Yes
Tranquilizers	Miltown,® Equanil,® Valium,® Thorazine,® Librium,® Noludar,® Placidyl®	Kill—uncommonly	Yes
Alcohol	liquor, beer, whisky, wine, "booze"	Kill—often	Yes
Stimulants†	amphetamines, Dexedrine,® Methedrine,® "bennies," "dexies," "speed," "meth," "uppers," "greenies," cocaine	Kill—rarely	Yes
Hallucinogens	LSD, STP, PCP, TCP, DMT, MDA, DMA, MDM, peyote, mescaline, psilocybin, morning glory seeds, "acid"	Kill—very rarely	Yes (? 3 days)
Cannabis	marihuana, hashish, THC, "pot," "grass"	Kill—extremely rare	Reverse
Vapors	kerosene, gasoline, glue, cleansing agents, aerosols	Kill—uncommonly	No
Tobacco	cigarettes, cigars, pipe, tobacco, snuff	Kill—very rarely	No

*Taken from: Bruce H. Woolley, Pharm. D., Director of Post Graduate Education, USC School of Pharmacy.

†Often "mainlined" or "shot-up" (taken intravascularly). Complications frequent— hepatitis, bacterial sepsis, bacterial endocarditis, thrombophlebitis, pulmonary embolism, pulmonary infarction, lung abscess, arteritis, gangrene, tetanus, sudden death (? cause) and others.

COMMON PSYCHOACTIVE DRUGS OF ABUSE*

DEPENDENCE		WITH-DRAWAL DISTRESS	OTHERS
MENTAL (Habituation)	PHYSICAL (Addiction)		
Yes	Yes	Yes	Sudden death. Pushing. Pimping. Prostituting. Property crimes.
Yes	Yes	Yes (most severe)	Mixtures potentiate effects (esp. alcohol). Convulsions.
Yes	Some-times	Sometimes	Chemical "copout". Convulsions.
Yes	Yes	Yes (severe)	Convulsions. Cirrhosis. Nerve & brain damage. Pancreatitis. Myopathy. Cardiomyopathy. Accidents. Homicide. Suicide. Work absences— G.I., Resp. & Musculoskeletal.
Yes	No	?	Psychoses (temp. or perm). Hypertension. Hypermetabolic state. Brain hemorrhage. Arteritis. Aggressiveness. Paranoia.
Yes	No	No	Psychoses (temp. or perm.). Bad trips. Irrational behavior. ?Chromosome abnormalities. Flashbacks.
Yes	No	No	Temporary psychoses. Flashbacks. ?Amotivation. ?Neuroses. ?Accidents. ?Delayed maturing. ?Gynecomastia.
Yes	No	No	Suffocation. Sudden death. Liver damage. Bone marrow damage.
Yes	Yes (early)	Yes	Emphysema. CA of many organs. Hearing & blood vessel diseases. Pregnancy problems. Skin wrinkling.

become quite disoriented, paranoid, and frightened. The "trip" lasts for four to twelve hours or up to a few days. One of the frightening aspects of the LSD trip is that it can suddenly recur weeks or months later.

Since different kinds of drugs obviously cause different kinds of reactions in the client, the client's responses and attitudes will be different depending on the type of drug he is on. The chart on the preceding pages describes the behavior traits caused by different drugs. It also lists nicknames or street names for the various drugs and the danger levels of each. The street names are important to the counselor in understanding the client's drug-related conversation. The danger levels are important information for the counselor for reference in possible medical emergency situations.

Having looked at the drug addict and his problem, we now turn to the alcoholic. The alcoholic addicts outnumber the drug addicts ten to one, and the alcoholic addicts tend to be older than the narcotic counterpart and have more money too. Of the estimated ten million alcoholics in the United States, only about three to five percent are the "skid row" type. The rest are scattered throughout the urban, suburban and exurban neighborhoods. About one-half of the country's alcoholics are employed; and unfortunately, all too many alcoholics are out on the streets and highways. As the Allstate® ad headlines, "One of the next 50 drivers coming your way is drunk. Not drinking — Drunk!" Two of every five people over the age of fifteen killed on the nation's highways die with a high alcohol content in their blood streams. A total of 55,000 people die in automobile accidents caused by drivers under the influence of alcohol each year.

In addition to the highway deaths, alcoholism kills 35,000 from homicides; 7,000 from suicides; and another 11,000 from the effects of the disease of alcoholism itself. Alcoholism is a disease of dependency upon drinking which causes a person to lose control over his normal ability to function in a reasonable way. It begins as social drinking and progresses through stages of growing psychological dependence followed by growing physical dependence. As time goes on, the incipient alcoholic begins to drink a little more and a little more to bring on the soothing effects that overcome the person's anxiety. Blackout periods begin to crop up, masking the person's recall of earlier events because of the alcohol's increasing blockage of oxygen to the brain, thereby short-circuiting the normal memory activity. Alcohol grows from a social context to an all-encompassing habit, a habit which begins to find its outlet with solo drinking and drinking with non-critical companions. Blackouts continue, and the incipient alcoholic grows more and more defensive about his drinking.

Somewhere along in here the victim slips from the initial stage into the middle stage, in which alcohol benders grow more and more common. The victim can still resist the initial drink; but once the sequence is begun, it now plays itself out through involuntary chain-drinking. Rationalizations and excuses fortify the victim now as he begins to lose his job, his family, and his friends. Signs of physical breakdown and malnourishment are showing up; and the alcoholic is now dependent upon the morning drink, which is taken as a cure for the past but becomes the beginning of a new chain of non-stop drinking.

The chronic stage brings the alcoholic to complete loss of control. Benders are now constant as the tolerance for alcohol decreases. Oblivion is never far away anymore, and neither is the rotten feeling of guilt and worthlessness. What becomes of the victim in his chronic stage of alcoholism? There are only three possibilities at this point: complete abstinence, insanity or death.

Somewhere along the way the alcoholic may come to a counseling service for information on alcoholism, help "for a friend" or advice for himself. He may or may not be drunk, but his call or visit to the counseling service proves he wants help, and the cry for help stems from the crisis impact of his situation. Whatever worked for the client up until now is not working anymore. He can no longer cope and that brings on a crisis situation in which he can no longer function normally.

The ABC Method works on substance abuse problems as well as other personal problems. The client himself must identify the problem, catalogue the options open to him, and ultimately, make his own choice from the list of alternatives that he, himself, has listed. The importance of this discussion of substance abuse (to repeat) is to underline the external effect that these chemicals have on the client's mind and hence on his thought process.

The counselor should determine if the client is on alcohol or drugs because that will provide a key to understanding what the client has to say about himself and his problem. The counselor should also bear in mind the physical and psychological reactions that can be expected from these addictions. And finally, the counselor should know which community resources can best help this client if he expresses a need for referral.

CHAPTER TEN

ETHICS AND LEGALITY

AN organized counseling service fills a serious need for the community, but it also carries with it some serious responsibilities. Without a solid ethical framework for its calling, the counseling service will quickly lose the respect of the client and the confidence of the community. Without solid legal framework, the service will lose its right to help the client. In either case, the client and the community are the losers when a badly-needed service, staffed by well-meaning counselors, becomes crippled by problems brought on by relaxed ethical or legal standards.

The ethics of a counseling service are the professional standards by which the counselors "do right by the client." Every profession is bound by a strong set of ethics, recognized by all of its respectable members and adhered to religiously. The medical and legal professions and the clergy all have sets of rigid ethical standards which doctors, lawyers and ministers uphold at all costs, even though the easy way out might often be to fudge a bit on a rule. Paraprofessional or nondegreed counseling has the same kind of ethical standards which help make sure that the client's privacy is protected.

One of the key principles of a counseling service is the principle of confidentiality. The name and background of a client are kept in locked, confidential files. The files are available to the staff members so that the client can be assisted on return visits whether or not the original counselor is present at the time. The client's file is a matter of strict confidence between himself and the counseling service. It cannot be released to anyone else without the written, signed, and dated permission of the client.

What if a concerned member of the family asks to see the record? How about a helpful parent or thoughtful wife? No!

Can a counseling service share the record with the client's own physician or psychiatrist or social worker? *Absolutely not.* How about the client's minister, priest or rabbi? Still NO!

All of these people might sincerely want to help. And maybe they are just the people who can and will help. Maybe the client wants them to help by reviewing his record. But remember, the client must sign a written, dated release form before any non-staff member can see his file.

The confidentiality of the client's case extends to revealing that the client has called upon a particular counseling service. Suppose a physician called to ask for a client's file. He or she would have to be told that all files are confidential; and even the existence of a file is not something that the service is at liberty to discuss without the client's written, signed and dated permission.

Can the client's file be reviewed by other staff members for the purpose of familiarization and training. Yes, it can. It must be available to other staff members so that their professionalism can be strengthened by studying the range of cases handled by the service.

This should be no secret to the client though. In fact, there should not be any secrets from the client. The best kind of relationship with a client is an "up-front," honest relationship. When a client is reluctant to give out information about himself, the counselor should reassure him that his file is kept locked and confidential and can only be referred to by the professionals at the service (including paraprofessionals), either in helping the client or familiarizing themselves with the client's case. The client should further be told that there are only two circumstances under which information can be released to others outside the center: (1) when a human life is in danger, whether the client's or another person's, or (2) when the client himself expressly authorizes such a release in writing.

Not only the client's actual file, but the knowledge and discussion of his file, should be left in the counseling office. The counselor must leave his own — and the client's — problems at the center and not bring them up elsewhere. Cocktail party chatter about the case, even when the client's name is carefully masked, is a violation of the counselor's ethics. Perhaps the person being told of the case can still recognize a friend or relative. And even if the client's identity cannot be known, the listener is bound to think less of a counselor who is so loose about somebody else's very real problems. The reputation of the counselor and the agency is damaged by telling such tales "out of school."

It should be pointed out that the client's sensitivity to the file usually comes after the original call. At the time of the crisis call for help, information was given willingly to try to get help for the problem, but days, and weeks and months later, the client sometimes begins to have second thoughts about having allowed that information to be included in a file in an office somewhere. When a client calls to express such a concern, the counselor should assure the client of the confidentiality of the file and the conditions under which it could be released to others. Obviously, if the client asks to have the file destroyed, it should be destroyed.

No recordings should be made of the conversation, whether a phone or in-person interview, without the client's permission. No other staff member should listen in to the conversation without the client's permission. In many states it is illegal for third parties to listen to a phone conversation without the knowledge of either of the primary parties — except on a regular extension line in which the mouthpiece of the phone is in regular working order (not removed or tampered with). But whether or not eavesdropping is illegal, it is certainly unethical in a counseling situation.

Aside from ethical considerations of a paraprofessional or non-degreed counseling service, there are legal questions which can have serious consequences if ignored. Good intentions are no excuse for breaking the law or causing a law suit to ruin a good thing.

Help is a two-way street. People call on hotlines and walk-in counseling services for help, and the services should call for help too. One of the very first calls should be to an attorney. This chapter should not be taken as authoritative legal advice, but it might be helpful in pointing out areas of legal concern about which your new or old service should seek competent legal counsel.

There are four primary reasons why a counseling service needs an attorney: (1) liability, (2) organization, (3) accounting and (4) insurance. All too many counseling services figure that a lawyer is just one more hassle; and they launch right into business with a couple of telephones or desks, a group of volunteers and a lot of good will. That is a naive approach in a formal, structured society like this; and the euphoria could easily end with a scary lawsuit in six figures or with an official call by the Internal Revenue Service. It isn't fair to an organization's clients, volunteers, board or staff to run that kind of risk.

A service should take first things first and get some sound legal advice before it starts out (or right now if it is already operational and hasn't gotten around to it). What kind of attorney should a service seek? There are as many kinds of attorneys as there are social agencies; some are more suited to a counseling operation's concern than others. The best kind of lawyer for this purpose is a business attorney. It's not that the service is going to be sharing business' profit-headaches, but, whether the service had thought of it that way or not, it will be sharing business' organizational headaches. It doesn't really matter so much whether the attorney is part of some large corporate structure or is a corporate attorney in private practice. A trial lawyer isn't always the best help to a counseling service since that kind of counsel isn't necessarily oriented to organization.

An organization can name the attorney to its board of directors, but it's not really necessary. It all depends on the purpose of the board and the function of its members. Generally, it isn't wise to fill a board membership for a limited function. It may be more appropriate for the service simply to seek an attorney who will offer his or her services as a volunteer.

The attorney will need to provide several recommendations at once: First of all, what formal structure should the organization assume and secondly, what about liability? Organization is a pain to many people who are busy getting a counseling service off the ground since they are anxious to shortcut the traditional bureaucratic structure and accomplish tangible results right away. They are motivated by a desire to help others, not a desire to build empires. But face it! To do very much good beyond one person's own capabilities, a lot of other people are needed to pull together in the same direction. And lots of people equal an organization .... an organization subject to special laws, taxation, regulation by various governmental agencies, and eligible for everything from juicy financial grants to horrendous law suits.

The moral is to organize soundly so that the service can go about its real mission of helping others unfettered by the problems of poor organization. As far as taxation goes, an organization is not generally tax deductible to its contributors until declared so by the state. In other words, the organization has an obligation to formalize its tax exempt status in government files.

Should a counseling organization incorporate or not? There is no universal answer to that; like so many things in the legal arena .... it all depends. There are advantages and disadvantages to both, and which is best for any given counseling service depends generally on the size of the organization's budget. Above a given amount, the organization should incorporate; and below that, it has a choice. In some states that figure might be $5,000; and in other states, a different amount.

Once the organization has incorporated, it will probably need to file an annual report if the funding is above a certain level. A good accountant will be needed then more than ever — plus good figures! At this point the organization probably becomes a corporation number in the state's files and will need to submit whatever paperwork is required each year. The two primary advantages to incorporation are: (1) to limit the liability of individual members and (2) to take advantage of corporation law with its helpful delineation of the rights of members and the duties of its officers.

The second immediate question that needs an attorney's attention is that of liability. Whether the organization is incorporated or not, liability is a major concern. Let's begin with the obvious. Suppose the counseling service has a Flying Squad, as many do, which responds to calls for help such as those from clients who have "OD'd" (overdosed) on drugs. Now, suppose the Flying Squad bursts into the wrong apartment after a call for help from an "OD'd" caller. The counseling service would be liable. Or suppose the Flying Squad was involved in an accident. The counseling service would be liable.

Okay, so a counseling service doesn't have a Flying Squad? How could it be liable then? Well, suppose one of the volunteers (who doesn't have insurance, as it turns out) is in an accident while going out to buy sandwiches for the other volunteers: The organization is liable.

Maybe a service thinks, naively, that it can somehow avoid all liability. It avoids the gray areas of a Flying Squad by avoiding such a service, and it issues strict instructions that no staff member is authorized to leave the premises on business of the organization, and that travel to and from the organization's site is strictly on the staff member's own time. The organization's staff carefully inspects the facility to make sure that the ceiling won't collapse and that no equipment could cause injury. Unfortunately, liability can be completely out of the control of the organization. One could hypothesize into infinity on the possible occurrences; but just to illustrate, suppose some mad man breaks into the building (despite all of the elaborate security precautions) and rapes a staff member who happens to be a minor — her parents might very well sue.

The answer to liability possibilities is insurance — the right kind in the right amount. If the organization is not incorporated, then liability insurance covering volunteer drivers while on the organization's business, and premises liability insurance for regular staff work might be advised. The better insurance that staff members have on their own, the safer the organization itself. It is also generally true that the director of a counseling service has much more chance of a suit than the individual members. Insurance is the best course for a nonincorporated counseling service, but incorporation is the only way to avoid 100 percent chance of individual liability.

The attorney should check the organization's written instructions and operating procedures very carefully in several areas especially. First, what is the counseling service's instruction on giving advice? Is the ABC Method to be followed religiously? If so, there should be no problem with medical or malpractice liability. But if a counselor should deviate and suggest any medical advice, the next call might be from the client's lawyer. Even a seemingly innocent, offhanded suggestion to "take a couple of aspirin and get some rest" might result in a law suit if that piece of medical advice results in harm to the client (which it conceivably could). Worse yet, imagine the consequences of recommending sleeping pills to a distraught client who might already have drugs in his system!

Actually, a client can file suit on anything that he and his attorney can imagine in terms of the counseling done by the organization, but as a rule, "good will" advice or service does not represent grounds for collection.

One of the key issues of ethics and legality for a counseling service is the matter of calling in the police. For a community counseling service good relations with the police are mandatory if the service is going to be a truly effective service to the people of the community. Generally speaking, there are only two holding agents that are allowed by law to detain a person against his will, and those two are the police and mental health authorities. In some states a licensed physician can sign detention papers. In any case, the staff of the counseling service should meet with police officials at the first opportunity to explain the counseling organization's purpose and operating procedures and to explore, in advance, the various areas where the counseling service and the police might share a concern or be involved together. The police are generally the only agency in town authorized to "bust down the door" to get to a client in the process of attempting suicide or a client that has passed out from a toxic level of drugs. The police should understand, though, that the counseling service is bound by an ethical standard (usually backed up by legal protection) to guard the confidentiality of its client contacts. Many of the client problems will relate to crimes committed or crimes contemplated. Clients may include child molesters, sexual deviants, rapists, burglars, muggers, dope dealers, and other types of law breakers being sought by the police. But the ethics of the service are concrete. The service exists for the client alone. There in only one exception to this rigid confidentiality between the service and client: *when human life is endangered.* When suicide or homicide are imminent, the police should and must be brought in. But again, this is the only exception to the pledge of secrecy that protects the counselor-client relationship in the paraprofessional or non-degreed service.

CHAPTER ELEVEN

THE BUILDING BLOCKS OF
A COUNSELING SERVICE

THIS final chapter is about bringing it all together: bringing volunteers together, training them, patching into the various community resources, and giving guidance to the administrator and board of directors. To make the ABC Method work for any kind of community, there must be an organization that runs smoothly and is available when people with problems need it.

Traits of a Good Counselor

First of all, what kind of person makes a good counselor? To me, there are six qualities that characterize a good counselor:

1. *Dependability.* Good intentions are great, but they don't help much if the counselor doesn't show up for a shift. You need a counselor that is as good as his word, who takes the training and can be counted on to be on the job as promised.

2. *For Real.* A person who comes across as a phony isn't going to be trusted by a client. Your counselor needs to be genuine and "up-front," and come across during counseling pretty much as he is in everyday, non-counseling situations. Beware of the person who slips into a new personality for the counseling job. He's role-playing and play-acting. Obviously a counselor can't be "totally for real" because that would mean sharing with the client a lot of hostility, prejudices and anger that have no part in a counseling dialogue. Use common sense. Look for a counselor who's "for real," not phony.

3. *Empathy.* Empathy means really caring about the other person's problems. It means identifying with the client, not just listening. It means involving yourself with the client's problems. A counselor must keep "playing back" what he understands of the problem to let the client know just how tuned in he is to the

64

client's dilemma. In a counseling situation, empathy must be felt and expressed.

4. *Warmth.* Warmth is hard to describe, but easy to recognize. With warmth a counselor can convey empathy and being "for real." Warmth is more than words; it reflects behavior traits .... both verbal and nonverbal. Without it, he's a cold fish; and regardless of how bright and capable he might be in other situations, he won't prove very effective as a counselor.

5. *Respect.* Respect is the most important characteristic of all. Is the client a "grossly overweight, immature misfit who sees fault in everything but himself", or is the same client "a fellow human with inherent worth, unrecognized abilities, and just as much right to make his choices in life as anyone else?" It all depends on the amount of respect the counselor has for the client. Respect cannot be turned on and off. Either you recognize every client's human worth and rights to his own decisions about how he will live his own life .... or you do not. A Navy admiral once asked a lowly ensign what the attitude of an ensign toward an admiral should be. "Respect," replied the ensign quickly. "And what should the attitude of an admiral be toward an ensign?", the admiral continued. The ensign gave the question some thought; then replied, "Exactly the same .... respect." The point is that a fellow human being is turning to a counselor for help. Neither is worth any more than the other, both have problems and fears. The counselor who recognizes that all-important truth is showing respect.

6. *Stability.* A counselor should have his own life pretty well in order before involving himself in the problems of others. He should feel content with who he is and where he is going. Counseling others means sharing some painful experiences. The client is a vessel adrift, seeking a solid foundation as a place to drop anchor. It doesn't help much to become anchored to another drifting vessel. If a person is going through a period of personal crisis, make sure that crisis can be set aside completely during periods of counseling.

Most of the people who volunteer to serve as paraprofessional counselors will probably have these six basic traits or they

wouldn't be interested in helping through this channel. It is for-
tunate that that's the case because there never seem to be enough
volunteers, and being able to accept most of the applications is a
happy circumstance. But be wary of the person who doesn't mea-
sure up to basic qualities. You're running a counseling organization to help problems, not spread them. If a candidate looks weak
for this challenge, tell him so respectfully and find another.

Training

Training is important to the success of a paraprofessional program. Once a group of volunteers has been chosen, a training
program should be launched to prepare them for counseling service. I know of new counseling services that have spent twelve
months or more training their volunteers before opening for business. That's too long. Think of the needs of that community that
were ignored by a full year's preparation. Six or eight lengthy
sessions should be the maximum number of training sessions for
a new counselor. Those could take place on a one-evening-a-week
basis, on weekends or in a daily sequence, depending on the
makeup of the group and the availability of its volunteers.

Use this book as a textbook, following the chapter headings for
subjects. Devote at least half of each session to role-playing. If the
counselors are being prepared for telephone counseling, then
telephones should be used in the training. It's possible to wire two
old telephones together so that you can actually converse over
them, even though you're back to back in the same room. Phones
are often donated by local telephone companies. If not, they can
be purchased inexpensively from firms in large cities which sell
used telephones.

The importance of role-playing can't be overemphasized. A
new counselor builds confidence in himself and in the system
through trying it out. Don't be afraid to challenge the ABC
Method by throwing curves into the role-playing interviews. In
fact, every role-playing problem should be made as difficult as
possible to serve as a challenge to the person playing the role of
the counselor, and as a reassurance to the person playing the role
of client that the system really does work in all situations.

By making the role-playing situations as challenging as possible, the trainees will be pleasantly surprised at how simple and routine most of their first calls will be. Prepare for the worst: The routine crises will seem commonplace.

Referral and Community Resources

One of the most important elements of running a paraprofessional counseling service is *referral*. People will call or walk in with every sort of problem. Many of those problems can be dealt with by professionals or paraprofessionals of other specialized agencies. There are agencies for alcoholics, drug abusers, marital problems, chronic emotional problems, women with unwanted pregnancies, compulsive gamblers, people who are overweight and so forth.

There's more to a referral than finding a phone number. First of all, as was emphasized in earlier chapters, do not suggest an assistance agency until the client expresses a need. Maybe he doesn't want an agency to help him. Maybe he's tried agencies before and is calling you to help work out his problems on his own. On the other hand, don't cut the ABC interview sequence short by responding directly to an early question about agencies. Talk through the problem, using the ABC Method, until you are convinced that the client's problem and needs are such that they would be well served by an agency.

If the referral comes with the client's first call, offer assistance in making the connection with the other agency. Don't just dispense a phone number and forget about it. If the client has been calling and coming in for periodic counseling and you and the client have agreed that an agency with more specific resources would be in the best position to help him, take extreme care in the transfer of the client from your service to theirs. Don't leave him in the no-man's land in between agencies. Think for a moment about the feelings of the other agency: There may be the feeling you are simply flushing an unwanted problem its way. Or there might be a sense of flattery that you referred a client to their particular agency. Or there might be a mixture of both. Remember that the new agency does not yet have the feeling of commitment towards

Agency Name:_____Smithville Free Clinic_____

Address:_____1201 Main St._____

Phone:____576-4182_____   Director:_____Dr. Florence Gayle____

Services Provided: ____(1) Non-emergency medical care for needy_____

(2) Pregnancy tests   (3) Abortions   (4) Free Baby Clinic (Thurs.)

Fees: __Based on ability to pay.   Hours: 9 am − noon, Mon.−Sat.____

Restrictions: __Clients must certify financial need.   Open_____

mornings only._____

Visited by: ___M. A. R.   Date: 3/2/74   Talked to: Angie Lopez, Asst. Dir.

Information confirmed (date):____8/17/75_____

The cross-reference card might look like this:

```
┌──────────────────────────────────────────────────┐
│                                                    │
│   PREGNANCY                                        │
│                                                    │
│              Smithville Free Clinic                │
│                                                    │
│                                                    │
│                                                    │
│                                                    │
│                                                    │
│                                                    │
│                                                    │
└──────────────────────────────────────────────────┘
```

(Use a separate card for each "Pregnancy" cross-reference.)

this particular client that you have. You have a responsibility to the client throughout the transfer process and for a long enough period afterwards to insure that a successful transfer has been completed and that the client is getting the help he needs.

The client has come to trust you; now he is faced with starting all over, spilling his life's story one more time to a new name and face. He'll need your help and encouragement as he gets it on with his new agency. And remember, you are prohibited by law, ethics and common sense from transferring your records of the client to a new agency without his *written* advance permission.

As a counseling service you must know of all of the agencies of the community whose services might be available to your clients. Your list of community resources may well number into the hundreds, so it's important that the full details of each agency be verified, organized for easy reference by the individual counselors, and reverified periodically.

A card file is perhaps the easiest way to organize the information on community resources so that information can be easily added or corrected. Each community resource should be filed under its formal name. Duplicate cards should be made out for each of the major problems handled by that agency. For example, duplicates of the card for "Smithville Free Clinic" might be filed under "Physician," "Clinic," "Pregnancy," "VD" and "Baby Medical Care."

The form on each individual agency might look like the form on page 68.

How does a new counseling service go about finding what community resources are available? First of all, split up the job among all of the counselors. If each counselor visits a few agencies, all will have a greater appreciation of what services are performed for clients at specialized agencies. Secondly, consult the overall community organizations: city hall, police department, chamber of commerce, city library. Perhaps partial or comprehensive lists of services have already been compiled in some form. Using those lists as skeletons, send your fingers on a trip through the yellow pages under the headings of marriage counselors, clinics, psychiatrists, hospitals, emergency services, etc.

For starters, you should have referral agencies in mind for at least these categories:

Aged

Alcoholism

Asian-American

Baby medical care

Black

Blind

Child day care

Child psychiatrist

Clinic

Day care

Drugs

Emergency, medical

Emergency, psychiatric

Family services

Financial problems

Gambling

Gay service

Hearing

Hospital

Indian

Legal assistance

Marriage counseling

Medical (see emergency, physician
      or speciality)

Narcotics (see drugs)

Overdose (see emergency medical)

Overweight

Physically handicapped

Physician

Pregnancy

Psychiatrist

Psychologist

Rape

Retardation

Schools — special education

Sexual problems

Social worker

Spanish speaking

V.D.

Welfare questions

Women

Administration

Now a few tips for the administrator. Believe everything you
have ever read about leadership. Whether you're leading an in-
fantry unit or a Big Sur commune, the principles are the same. If
the organization is going to function as a cohesive organization
and achieve the goals it has set for itself, it is going to need sound
leadership; and the principles of leadership are rather constant. In
short, leadership is where the buck stops. The leadership is where
the ultimate decisions are made. Leadership is the inspiration and
example to the rest. Leadership is the coordinator of activities.
Like it or not, leadership is the boss.

If you are the administrator, set your sights firmly on the goal of
your organization. Perhaps it is to make available twenty-four-
hour-a-day telephone counseling to a certain geographic community. Perhaps it is to offer walk-in counseling on a face-to-face

basis to a certain community or group. Whatever it is, set your goal and make it achievable and very specific. With your goal firmly in mind at all times, a lot of minor decisions can be made routinely. For example, you're being asked to speak to a business-men's group in a community fifty miles away. Since your service does not serve that community, and there is no possibility for funds deriving from that speaking engagement, perhaps your half a day might be better spent on something that directly helps achieve your goal.

Your relationship with your counselors must be friendly (of course); but you cannot be the administrator and "one of the gang" at the same time. Like it or not, those are the facts. And just as inevitably, you've got to adjust yourself quickly to the fact that you're not going to be universally loved and respected. Some will resent your leadership. Some will disagree with some of your decisions. Some won't like your leadership style. Pay attention to those grievances, but don't be stymied by them. Those are the prices paid for sticking your neck out and getting the job done. Be firm and fair, and keep plugging towards the goal. You'll make it.

Remember this critical fact: as administrator, you are just that. Your job is to manage. If someone doesn't show up for his shift, find someone else to fill in; don't take over the job yourself. All of the time you spend doing someone else's job is time you've taken away from the administrator's job. You can't possibly do every-one's job, so limit yourself to your own. Make sure there are back-up people and systems. Use your time to organize, raise funds, form liaisons with other community services, and find new counselors.

Perhaps the two most important things to remember about volunteers is (1) don't work them too hard and (2) reward them with praise and recognition every chance you get. The first seems to contradict logic. If a volunteer wants to put in a lot of time, why not let him? The reason is that he will become "burned out," and he'll get there faster than you would have dreamed possible. Counseling is a demanding job, and too much of it can force a volunteer to bail out in despair. Don't kill the goose to get the golden egg. If at all possible, limit every volunteer's involvement to once or twice a week — maximum. The second consideration is rather self-explanatory. We all like praise and recognition. If the newspaper is doing a feature on your service, try to get as many of the volunteers as possible mentioned by name. Have the Board recognize the volunteers formally once a year at a dinner, if possible. Reward them in any way you can. Without them you're no organization at all!

Board of Directors

What is a Board of Directors and why have one? In having a board of directors formed, an administrator is having bosses set up over him. There is an obvious risk in that since one is freer without a board looking over one's shoulder. But the fact is, you probably need a board. If your service is one which serves a community, then you'll need dozens of volunteers, a few telephones, an office somewhere and an endless stream of necessities that begin to add up to big money. It can cost thousands, or even tens of thousands of dollars to operate a counseling service — even when volunteers are used to doing the counseling.

The board of directors will not be involved in the day-to-day operation of the service, but they do assume responsibility for the overall direction and success of the operation. If you are a community organization, you should find the most influential community members who will agree to be members of your board. Your appeal to them will obviously point out the great need for the service and the opportunity to provide this service at a relatively inexpensive cost. Your board members need to be those who have money and/or access to money. An effective board will raise those thousands, cement relations with other influential community organizations and free the administrator to run the service on a day-in-day-out basis.

A good rule to remember is not to clutter your board with people whose services you are after. If you want legal services volunteered, ask the attorney for the services. If you want advertising or public relations help, ask someone to contribute those services. Save the board chairs for people whose thoughts and voices count in the community you are serving. As to the number of members for your board, about a dozen ought to do it.

That's enough advice. You now know how a non-professional can use the ABC Method to counsel other people in need. And you know something about organizing ABC-trained counselors into a service that can make a difference in your community, your agency, your prison, your Navy frigate or your school.

Now set the book down and get started!

INDEX

A

ABC Method, 6-7, 16-21
 A is for Acquiring, 16-19, 22-27
 B is for Boiling Down, 16, 18-19, 28-33
 C is for Coping, 16, 19-21, 34-38
 reduction of tension, 17
 substance abuse problems, 55-56
Accounting problems, 59, 61
Acquiring information about client, 16-
 19, 22-27, 34
 homicidal client, 47
 nonverbal clues, 18
 questions asked, 18
 verbal clues, 18
Administrator's role and function, 70-72
Advice-to-a-friend method, 40
Advice to client, 11-12, 34-35
Alcohol, 49, 52-53 (Table)
Alcoholics, 54
 number of, 48, 54
 types, 54
Alcoholism, 48, 54
 blackouts, 54-55
 chronic stages, 55
 stages in, 54-55
Alternative solutions open to client, 36
Amphetamines, 51
Anxiety, 18, 22, 29
 relief of, 22, 25
"Anxiety Overheat" light, 10
Assault and battery, 46
Attorney
 board of directors member, 60
 needs for, 59-60
 type needed, 60

B

Background noise, 18
Barbiturates, 51

"Bennies," 51
Benzadrine, 51
Board of directors, 72-73
 attorney as member, 60
Boiling down information from client,
 16, 18-19, 28-34
 homicidal client, 47
Breathing rate, 18
Building blocks of a counseling service,
 64-73
Burglars, 63

C

Cannabis, 52-53 (Table)
Change in life situation, 30
Child-battering, 46
Child molestation, 46
Child molesters, 63
Chronic complainer, 19
Clergy, aid of, 9
Clients, types of, 63
Cocaine, 49-50
Codeine, 49
"Cold turkey" drug cures, 50
Community resources, 69-70
 categories of, 70
Conclusion of interview, 39
Confidentiality of client's files, 57-59
 exception to, 63
Conversation by client, importance of, 28-
 29
Coping with situation, 16, 19-21, 31, 34-
 38
Coughing, 18
Crisis, determining existence of, 19
Crying, 18

D

"Dangerous drugs," 49, 51

75

Dependability, 64
Depressants, 51
Depression, 29
Detention of clients, 63
Dexadrine, 51
"Dexies," 51
Dope dealers, 63
Drug addiction, 48

E

Eavesdropping on telephone conversations, 59
Empathy, 26, 64-65
Ethical standards of counseling service, 57-59

F

Family physician, aid of, 9
Flying Squad, 61-62
Friends, aid of, 9
Freud, Sigmund, 3

G

Genuineness, 64
Goal of client, arriving at, 40-41
Goal setting for client, 35
"Goofballs," 51

H

Hallucinogens, 49, 51-53 (Table)
Heroin, 49-50
 cost, 50
Heroin client, characteristics of, 50
Homicidal cases, 34
Homicidal clients, 5, 46-47
 acquiring information about, 47
 boiling down information from, 47
 hospitalization of, 47
 psychiatric evaluation of, 47
Homicidal problem, 29
Homicidal tendencies, indicators of, 46
Homicide, 49
 police brought in, 63
 rate of, 46
Human contact, 22

I

Identifying information, 23
Illustrative dialogues with clients, 5, 7, 13-15, 20-21, 23-24, 26-27, 30-33, 37-38
Incorporation of counseling service, 61
 advantages of, 61
Instructions of counseling service, 62
Insurance problems, 59, 62
Interpersonal problems, 29
Intuition, use of, 26
Inventory of coping in past, 35-38
Isolation of client's exact problem, 28

J

"Jehovah Complex," 11

L

Leadership, principles of, 70
Legal framework of counseling service, 57-63
Liability problems, 59, 61-62
Life-and-death situation, 5, 42
Loss of balance, 36
Loss of control, 30
Loss of dependency, 30
LSD, 51, 54

M

Marijuana, 49-51
Medical paraprofessional, 8
Mental problems, 29
Mental vertigo, 36
Morphine, 49
Muggers, 63
Multiple solutions, 40

N

Name of client
 importance of, 24
 request for, 23-24
Narcotics, 52-53 (Table)
 persons addicted to, 49
New adjustment in life, 30
Nonverbal clues, 18, 25

O

OD'd clients, 61
Operating procedures, 62-63
Opiates, 49
Opium client, characteristics of, 50
Opium cost, 50
Organization of counseling service, 59-61

P

Paraprofessional counseling (*see also*
  ABC Method *and other specific topics*)
advice to client, pitfalls of, 11-12
function, 4-5
help provided by, 10
helping client to cope on his own, 13-15
how it works, 8-15
life-and-death problems, 5
method of, 8-15
need for, 3, 42
peer level of, 4
psychological vs. medical, 8
role of, 3-7
solution of client's problem, pitfall of,
  11-12
successes of, 42
supplement to professional counseling,
  4
support of client, 20
24-hour service, 4
Paraprofessional counselor
administration, 70-72
board of directors, 72-73
community resources, 69-70
referral, 67-69
training, 66-67
traits of, 64-66
Pauses, 18
"Pep pills," 51
Physical problems, 29
Play-acting, 64
Police, good relations with, 63
Precipitating stress
determination of, 19, 29-30
types, 30
Preteen callers, 5
Problem-solving ability of client, 35-36
Problems of clients, 29

Professional standards, 57
Pseudo-gripes, 28
Pseudo-problems, 28
Psychedelic drugs, 51
Psychoactive drugs of abuse, 52-53 (Table)
Psychological paraprofessional, 8

R

Rapists, 63
Rapport with client, 18, 22, 25-26
Reassurance of client, 24
Recordings of interviews, permission for,
  59
Referral services, 67-69
Refusal to divulge name and phone
  number, 24-25
Relatives, aid of, 9
Respect, need for, 65
Responsibilities of counseling service, 57
Role-playing, 6, 64, 66-67

S

Schizophrenic client, 25
Secrecy, pledge of, 63
Sedatives, 52-53 (Table)
Sex crimes, 46
Sexual deviants, 63
"Shrinker vs shrinkee" society, 3
Sighs, 18
Solution of client's problem, 11-12
client's vs. counselor's, 12, 39
methods of arriving at, 39-40
Stability, 65
Stimulants, 51-53 (Table)
Substance abuse, 48-56
Suicidal calls, 5
Suicidal cases, 34
Suicidal clients, 42-47
actual taking of life by, 46
alternative actions, 45
medical emergency, 44
method to be used by, 44-45
nature of, 44
reason for, 45
seriousness of threat, 44-45
shock value in handling of, 44-45

Suicidal problem, 29
Suicide, 49
  candidates for, 43
  myths about, 43-44
  police brought in, 63
  rate of, 43, 46
Sympathy to client, 12

T

Taxation problems, 60-61
Telephone hot lines, 5-6, 10-11
Telephone number of client, importance
  of, 24
Timetable for goal, 40
Tobacco, 52-53 (Table)
Traditional sources of strength, lack of, 9
Training requirements, 66-67
Traits of good counselor, 64-66

Tranquilizers, 52-53 (Table)
Transfer of records, permission for, 69

U

"Up-front" relationship with client, 58-64

V

Vapors, 52-53 (Table)
Variations in techniques, 26
Verbal clues, 18

W

Walk-in, face-to-face counseling centers,
  7, 10-11
Warmth, 65
Withdrawn client, 25